BROKEN
FOUNDATION

"Adversity Is Not The Destiny"

Coach John M. Knapp

Published By: Books For Athletes
www.BooksForAthletes.com

TABLE OF CONTENTS

BROKEN FOUNDATION

*"Strength does not come from winning. Your struggles develop your strengths. When you go through hardships and decide not to surrender, that is strength." - **Gandhi***

This game of life comes with no instructions. No matter how well you prepare for it, the outcome isn't usually controlled by us. Some things are meant to be, while the rest, well, you sort of wing it in hopes that it turns out in your favor. Trial and error are pretty much the best way that I can put it. Because when it came to my life, I had no idea it was going to turn out as great as it did. There were times when I used to sit down and envision what my future would be like given the struggles I once faced as a child. Although I never fully understood the situations, we were in growing up, I knew they weren't that great. When I reminisce about my childhood, I have realized that I have really come a long way. There were many bumps and bruises along the way, but giving up just wasn't in me. I wasn't as fortunate as many of the other children from my neighborhood and although at times I wished I had as much as they did, I wouldn't trade in any of my experiences for different results. I might not have known it at the time, but life was preparing me for the roles that I would be playing later as an adult. As a tool, I began to use all of my struggles, all of my pain and any regrets I was still holding on to and using it to help others. To put it in better terms, I took the good with the bad and turned it all into a positive.

Growing up, I was the type of child who people would say was small, energetic, very athletic and was always seeking attention. There was just so much going on in my early life. All I was concerned with as I got older was getting out of my parents' house as soon as I could because of how dysfunctional it was living with them. I know that there are going to be many of my former players and students that will probably read this story and be very shocked to hear about the many obstacles I had gone through as a child. They'll be even more surprised that they really didn't stop there. Because even though life as a teacher and a coach were both great experiences, I continued to face many battles and situations that seemed like they were never going to end. Part of life is to try and figure out what your purpose is. Why am I here? What are we here to accomplish? Or even a better question: why me? Why was it that I had to be placed in so many crucial situations where I had to be the one to struggle while trying to figure out the best ways to solve them? I had many of my own issues growing up where I felt were very unfair. Although my parents stayed together until I was eighteen years old, the only thing I felt I learned from them was to never become how they were when I grew up. And this is not me taking a shot at my parents. Now that I am an adult, I understand how no one's life is ever perfect and all you can really do is play with the deck of cards you were dealt with. But they did have choices to make when it came to trying to raise me the right way. They just always seem to care more about their own personal priorities which almost never had anything to do with me. If it wasn't because of their drinking or them arguing and at times putting their hands on each other, it was me feeling like I had to try to find a way to enjoy my life somehow. I had a few friends growing up. But what I really wanted was for my parents to love me.

My dad, Charles, was a painter. My mother, Mary, was a bartender and factory worker. And although they both worked many hours; one would think we should have had a stable home where the bills were always paid on time and our refrigerator was filled with food. That wasn't the case though. Between the ages of three and all the way up to eighteen, we practically lived in a total of seven houses where five of them were all in the same neighborhood. It seemed like every two years we were moving into a new home. None of it ever made any sense to me, but the only good thing about it was that I never had to change schools and would still be able to hang out with my childhood friends. Each one of those houses we lived at had their own stories which for the most part was pretty intense. The best memories I have from living in those houses were when we got to spend Thanksgiving and Christmas together as a family. If we weren't spending the holidays at our place, we would go down to my grandmother's house where all my cousins would show up and play with us. I would always get really excited when they came because it would take my mind off all the craziness that was going on between my parents. It took for me to become an adult and have conversations with some of my cousins to realize that the reason why they were never allowed to come over to play was because my parents were always feuding. That was very interesting to me because I had never thought about it that way. In fact, that would have probably never crossed my mind if they wouldn't have mentioned it to me. I guess when you're a younger child that your mind never wanders that far where you question things like that. But I do remember that as I got older, my parents treated each other worse as time went on. So, I could see why no one ever wanted to be around us. As time went on, it appeared my parents hated each other so much that they could no longer hold back from fighting in front of whoever was there. It seemed everyday was an episode between them.

I remember one day, I was maybe 10 or 11 years old, and I had heard my mother yelling loudly at the top of her lungs for whatever reason. I could sense that she was angry. Me, not knowing what was going on, I went and walked into the kitchen where the argument was taking place. When I looked up, I saw that my mother had my dad's mother in a choke hold over the stove. Good thing the stove was off because she would have probably burnt her entire back. I couldn't understand why that was going on or even begin to put together a good enough reason in my mind to make any sense out of it. Within two seconds, I saw my dad come running into the kitchen and smack my mother across her face so hard that my mother's nose was busted up bad. It was really frightening for me to have to see that happening. The only thing I thought about at that moment was to run and hide in my bedroom closet hoping and praying that the altercation would end. Oh, it ended alright. It ended with my father being handcuffed and taken away to jail after the police had been called. Then, there was another time during a family get together. This time it was at our house. I was running around in the front of the house and saw my grandmother, my mother's mom, had my dad dangling from his feet and a full grip around his neck while yelling, *"don't you ever touch or hit my daughter ever again in your life"*. Once again, I took a quick look and just kept on running around the house to play with my cousins. I just wanted it all to end. But things would only continue getting worse. Those types of situations would continue happening all the way until I was eighteen and old enough to finally move out. By that time, I had figured out that it wasn't just the liquor that played a big part in the reason why they were always going at it, but also the accusations of both taking turns cheating on each other.

Nothing ever made real sense to me back when I was a child. It was very difficult for me to understand the reasons why my parents fought so much, but it was very evident that they began to hate each other more and more each day. Although I was aware of that, I wasn't smart enough to figure out why my mother was always taking me to go watch men's softball games and the players were making me the bat boy. While watching them play and running around chasing foul balls all day was fun, my mother was cheating on my dad with some of those softball players. Again, I was a young kid, and the thought never crossed my mind. Then, when my mom would go work at the bar, I would see those same softball players walking around and I began to piece my thoughts together and was finally able to realize what my mother had really been up to. Of course, I wasn't comfortable with what she had been doing, but there was nothing I could say or do about it. But my father was no saint either. He was also cheating on my mother with other women too. There did come a small period when I believe they did try to make their marriage work. I could tell because everything became sort of peaceful. It was kind of shocking to me at the time, but it was better than what it had always been. My mother knew that her lifestyle and working at the bar was becoming an issue, so she moved on and started working at a local factory called *United Dividers.* That was her way of trying reconcile with my father, by getting out of the bar scene. And things seemed to have become better between them. I was so happy because I didn't find myself having to run into the closet and hiding like I always did when they argued or fought. I saw a lot more family unity and experienced some positive times, but something happened at the factory which caused her to go back into the bartending life. Soon after, everything began to snowball and go downhill all over again. Aside from my dad's painting job, he and my uncles were also working at, Elmira Heights American Legion as officers. My mom and her sister later became involved somehow and started working there too. Occasionally my cousin, David, and I would be asked to work there and clean up the place. I loved it because there were times, I would find a bunch of money they would allow me to keep. But that was short lived. Before you knew it, everyone began cheating on each other and eventually ended up becoming the end of everyone's marriage in my family. It was a tough time for me because all I had ever wanted was for everyone to be happy. But of course, that too was totally out of my control.

Everything seemed to really change for me when we ended up moving out of our neighborhood to Elmira Southside when I was fourteen years old and heading into the eighth grade. I had always wondered why we were constantly moving from house to house until one day, I overheard a discussion between my parents and was able to figure out the reason. From a kid's standpoint, almost every situation became very difficult for me to have to deal with because I never really knew why they ever occurred. My parents had always been the type to mismanage their money. While standing close to their bedroom door, I vividly remember hearing them going back and forth until one of them said *"we're moving"*. The reason behind us constantly moving from house to house was because they were always looking for a cheaper place they could afford. Anytime they realized they weren't going to be able to afford to pay the rent, they would go and look for another place. Only this time it was different though. Not only did I have to suck it up and deal with all my problems at home, but I also now had to attend a new school where I didn't know anyone. I had no say. That move was crushing for me because I had always been around all my closest friends and now, I had to adjust to a new environment. It was like entering the twilight zone. I didn't know a single student there.

I distinctly remember walking into *Parley Coburn Junior High School* as an eighth grader/ninth grader and looking around not recognizing anyone and being stared down by almost every student that walked past. Thank God for the teachers because they understood just how I was feeling. Of course, I didn't know at the time that I would later become a teacher myself and had to deal with similar situations with some of my new students, but the way those teachers took care of me also became my way of looking out for my own. I have always gravitated to a lot of the students to make sure they felt safe in their new environment. There were many adults who taught me how to treat others based on how they always treated me. I was a good kid. I wasn't really the type who was rude or went around starting trouble. And maybe that's part of the reason why everyone was always good to me. But moving to a new school was one of my hardest and scariest moments as a teenager .

It took me a while to get used to it. Even though I did have the opportunity to go back to my old school a year later, because my parents decided to move back to the Eastside yet again, I chose to stay at Parley Coburn Junior High because by then I had already made many new friends and was on the school's basketball, baseball and soccer teams. The only problem was Elmira Southside was about three and a half miles from our house and I now had to walk every day to get there. I know there are people who exaggerate stories about how long they had to walk to school, but I did have to walk that far. I distinctly remember having to take those long walks from the Southside down Madison Street while carrying a pillowcase with a string in it over my back that I used to use as a backpack. There were times my dad had painting jobs close to the school and would give me a ride or drop me off somewhere near it, but for the most part, I had to walk no matter the weather. There were also other times I would get lucky and catch a ride by one of the coaches who would always see me walking. I used to try to avoid him many times because I didn't want anyone to make it their responsibility where they felt they had to go out of the way to transport me back and forth to school. But Coach Senko, who was my junior varsity baseball coach at the time, was such a great guy and would always look out for me. He became my mentor and was the type to take you under his wing when he knew you needed a little hug. Then there was our business teacher, Mr. Kinney, who saw me walking one day and offered me a ride to school. I didn't know it at the time, but he happened to live in an apartment just down the street from me on Oak Street. He said to me *"if you ever need a ride just knock on my door, come inside and wait for me in the barber chair".* He had this cool old fashion barber chair that I often sat in while I waited for him to come down the stairs so we could leave for school. But after a while I just began to feel very uncomfortable getting rides by him because, again, I didn't want to make it anyone's responsibility to have to give me a ride every day. Any other time, I would just hitchhike depending on how tired I was. By the time I was a senior, I had a few friends who had their own car and would often take me home. It was tough for me. Unfortunately, these were the types of consequences I had to deal with because of my parents' issues. I prayed almost every night for the situation to get better at our house. I hated that every time my parents would get into a fight that there was always some type of punishment for me that I would also have to deal with. Luckily for me, things ended up working out well for me at Elmira Southside High School, especially because I was athletic and was able to make many friends that way. Playing sports made everything a lot easier for me because I was pretty good at them. Another reason why I stayed at Elmira Southside High School was because that's where I ended up meeting my girlfriend, Kathy, who I am still married to today. Had it not been for her and her parents, I really have no idea where I would be in life because there came a time when I felt I had to begin doing things I knew could get me in trouble if I was caught.

As you can already tell, I had a crazy childhood growing up. I can remember stories all the way back from when I used to eat sugar sandwiches or would have to stand in long lines waiting for powder milk, peanut butter, canned tuna, flour and eggs with my mother. As a child, you feel those things are normal and that's just the way life was when you had nothing better to compare it to. You don't really pay attention to any of the details, and you just go along with it. It wasn't until I began to get a little older that I started to see that we really had it bad. While everyone at school wore brand new sneakers and nice clothes, I had maybe two or three outfits that I would have to constantly wash or else I wouldn't have anything to wear. I used to always ask myself why it was that my parents seemed to have all the money in the world to go out bowling several times a week but never enough to buy me new things. It just didn't make any sense to me. How was it that my mother would wash all my socks which at times would have blood on them from when I used to scrape my toes through the holes I had on the bottom of my shoes, yet they never stopped to think I probably needed a new pair? Or, how about when they saw me wearing the same exact clothes every single day, did they ever care that I was being made fun of almost every single day by other children? The most important thing that a child ever wants to feel is that they are being loved. Why weren't those things ever important enough for them? Of course, I wasn't bold enough to ever ask my parents those types of questions, but that did bother me a lot.

There were many times when I felt life was so unfair to me compared to others around me. You would think that a parent's job would be to protect the innocence of a child as long as they could, so that their memories would have been mostly positive. But that wasn't the case for us. I often wondered why they spent so much money on their social lives, while their children were home wearing hand me down clothes, which rarely fit. I know that none of it was ever done on purpose. I just always felt they could have done a better job as parents to make sure we were safe and somewhat happy. But they were too caught up in their own personal lives and dealing with their own problems to the point where they stopped paying attention to what was happening back at home. It got to the point where I reached an age where I was beginning to feel abandoned and barely even cared for. So, I decided to take matters into my own hands to try and figure out ways to survive or to deal with my stress and my struggles. I can't tell you how many times I would be so hungry and there was nothing in our refrigerator left to eat. There was this bakery just down the street from where I lived called, Millbrook Bakery and there was also a factory called, Dairylee Milk Company. Every time I would walk past it on my way home, I could always smell the fresh bread being made. I can still smell it now as I think about it. The smell alone made me hungrier. But of course, I had no money to be able to afford to buy any of it. So, we came up with a great idea. It was risky, but it was worth it at the time.

My friends and I had figured out that the bakery always would set aside all the outdated cookies and cupcakes on a separate rack. We also knew that the milk company kept a separate rack for soon to be outdated juices and milk. I was fast back then, and I always knew that I could outrun any of the workers there at the bakery or milk company. So, after me and some of our friends finished playing a pick-up game of basketball, we would head down to the Millbrook Bakery and grab whatever we could then take off running. My only concern at the time was getting caught and having to deal with my father later when I got home. But I knew they would never catch me. After eating all the cookies and cupcakes we would head down to Dairylee Milk Company and take off running with whatever drinks they had set to the side on a rack. None of the workers ever did come try and chase us down because it just wasn't worth their time. Besides, they knew they would eventually have to throw everything out anyway because they would all soon expire. But they got smart one day. What they ended up doing was stack up a bunch of sour chocolate milk to the side knowing that we would come back again. And they got us too. After taking off with the milk, we ran off and jumped over the fence and began chugging it down. The workers could hear us spitting it all up from the other side and began laughing their asses off. Those were some of the kinds of things I had to do to keep myself from starving.

Then there was the time when I decided I no longer wanted to keep wearing the same clothes every day and looking the way I did. Although I am now an adult and really don't see the importance of having to impress anyone by the clothes or sneakers I wear, there was a lot of pressure that came with being a teenager back then. I wanted to look as good as the other students at our school. Appearance was big for us back then and I was feeling like I had to step it up a bit. I know I couldn't go to my parents about buying me new clothes because I already knew what the answer would have been. Although I knew I was playing with fire, because of how strict my parents were, I decided to just go and steal clothes at Danny Discount Department Store which was a local clothing store. It wasn't my idea to become a thief, but when a friend of mine taught me just how easy it was to get away with it, I felt the risk was worth taking. *"All you have to do is go into the dressing room and put the new clothes on under your clothes and walk out"*, he would tell me. I got away with it two or three times, but once the workers at the store began noticing that all we were always doing was coming in and leaving without ever purchasing anything, we began to look like shoplifters instead of customers. While you're stealing, you really don't think anyone is paying attention to what you are doing. You look up and if no one is looking, you just take it. Till this day I can still remember the feeling of the man who grabbed me by the back of my shirt and pulled me back into the store because he knew I had stolen some of their clothes. My parents were called and when they arrived at the store, they began yelling at me and calling me a thief. Even though I had been caught stealing and made me return the clothes, they did not know that I had an outfit I had hidden underneath my bed. It was my favorite outfit and there was no way I was bringing it back. As a teenager, you always felt like you had to fit in. When you're struggling that hard in life, it sort of makes you feel like you are the poorest family on earth. Especially when it comes to peer pressure. But I will never forget that outfit I kept because I had my freshmen school picture taken with it on.

As an adult, I have been a witness to many similar situations where some of my students and players have felt the same pressure I felt when I was their age. Although we were all in school to learn and get good grades, that sometimes became secondary while trying to be cool or popular came first. But that was all just a phase. While most of my peers went off to college to earn their degrees, most of my lessons for the career path I chose were learned in my dysfunctional home setting. It was very difficult for me to try and predict what my future life was going to be like for me when I was finally old enough to move out on my own. Mentally, I was exhausted. Physically I just wanted out. I had gone through way too much to stay living in that environment one more day past my graduation. I even remember waking up every morning and counting all the way down to the very last day when I would go out and begin my journey as an adult. Although I always had it rough, I always had hope and prayed that everything was going to turn out positive for me somehow. I didn't know how I was going to do it or even where to begin, but I knew I was ready.

I don't really like mentioning to anyone I grew up poor and less fortunate than others, but that's really what it was. However, looking back I do feel my parents did do the bare minimum and could have done a lot more than they did. There was never a time when they sat me down to see what path I wanted to take in life as far as a career. But had anyone ever told me that I would be teaching students and coaching athletes for the next thirty-one years I would have thought they were insane because that wasn't my venture. I must be honest and say that I had never planned for any of it. Although I was a decent baseball player growing up, I would have never imagined what life had in store for me. When I first started coaching high school baseball, I really had no idea what I was doing. Being a player and having to lead a team were two entirely different things. I knew it wasn't going to be easy but being that the school district felt I was good enough to be given the opportunity to lead a team as a coach, I knew that I was going to give it my all from day one. Throughout my story in this book, I will share many situations that will give you a better understanding of what it took for me to be able to last as long as I did as a baseball coach. Many people think sports is all about winning and having fun, but as you will see, there is a lot more to it than just sitting around calling the plays.

I know that there are many athletes out there that have probably gone through similar situations or far worse in their own lives than I ever did. But I wanted to share my story in hopes that I could shed some light on how some parent's negative behavior and lifestyles could have a long-term effect on their own children's future. Somehow, someway I was able to survive mine. I feel I must get my story out there. I know there are many students and athletes out there struggling and not knowing what to do or who to turn to for help. If I could save one child by sharing my journey, to me it's all worth it. I would love to help and save as many as I could, but knowing what I have been through, I know it's not an easy task. Now that I am on my own journey and have overcome many of those obstacles, I wanted to use my own life as proof that you can make it out and that there is a chance that everything will turn out to be positive one day. I am an example of that. I say I am an example because my life could have taken a turn for the worse due to all that anger and resentment that was built inside of me because of my parents. This story wasn't written for me to publicly embarrass my parents in any way. My goal is that this book to reaches the hands of either the parents who may be treating their children unfairly or to a student/athlete who is currently dealing with this type of behavior in their own lives who may read this and say to themselves "*I have to change for the better or this book inspired me and gave me hope"*. That's what I really want to accomplish. That's my mission.

FORK ROAD

*"What the caterpillar calls the end, the rest of the world calls a butterfly." - **Richard Bach***

Although I have many crazy memories of my parents and all that we went through, I have always kept in the back of my thoughts that if and when I had children myself, I would definitely treat them better than how I was treated. Aside from those types of situations, my dad did instill hard work in me. I just always knew that I wanted better for myself and planned to do everything I could to have a better life. I also wanted to make our last name better than what everyone had become accustomed to. That was very important to me. I wanted to buy my own house, do well with my finances, live a comfortable life and treat people well. Life is sort of a puzzle where you have to try to figure out where you fit and what is going to work for you. Growing up, I had no idea what core values were. When it came to my parents, I always wondered to myself, *"what were the truths from what they were telling me?"*. Because as a child, it's normal to always believe what they said. I can understand a few fibs and white lies here and there, but to be lied to for all those years as a child? There was no need for all that. If that were the case, then why choose to have children? Going back to the situation where I was always being taken to all those men's softball games, I didn't know any of those players. Obviously, my mother did. I felt I should have been at the park having fun and doing things I enjoyed while playing with my buddies, but instead, I felt like we lived at those softball games. The crazy thing was, my own dad didn't even play softball. So, who were we really there to cheer on?

Now that I am older and able to use my common sense and put everything together, I feel like I had been living a lie for most of my childhood. Yes, maybe they were trying not to hurt my feelings by keeping as far away from being able to figure out anything that was going on in their lives. I always did question whether my life was ever all that important to them. Would I have been able to listen through and deal with the truth? Probably not, but they could have always done better. Because my parents spent so much time drinking alcohol, lying and cheating on each other, it always limited me from being able to enjoy my childhood. It would have been nice to be able to enjoy my dad pushing me on the swings at the park or guiding me from behind as I learned how to ride a bike. But I was lucky if I ever got a hug or heard them telling me that they loved me because they were too busy living in their own lies.

One of the fondest memories I have as a youth was when I would go fishing with my dad and my Uncle Herb at Catharine Creek. That was a really happy and glorious time in my life. We would always wake up early in the morning to get ready and make a brown paper bag lunch before heading out. Uncle Herb was totally different from my dad. I had a great relationship with him. He was a straight and arrow type of guy who never had any children of his own. In fact, I still remember Uncle Herb taking me to Sears Department Store and buying me one of my first baseball gloves. It was a Ted Williams glove, and I had that baseball glove all the way up until I was a freshman in high school. I really wished my dad and I had continued building a tighter relationship as a father and son, but it never turned out to be that way. Of course, many people will say *"well John, you have to just suck it up and move on, all of that is in the past"* but was it fair to me that most of my childhood memories must involve so much negativity which still brings some tears to my eyes? Through my struggles, I always believe that God had plans for me. I never knew what they were going to be at the time, but I always thought to myself *"something's gotta give one day".* I was a little scared because as I got closer to my graduation, I knew that my own life as an adult was going to soon begin. And boy let me tell you, that was a scary feeling. Although I wanted to go and live out on my own, I really had no idea what life had in store for me.

When I was a junior in high school, I remember having a conversation with a friend of mine who had mentioned to me that St. Josephs Hospital in Elmira was hiring. I felt it would be a great idea for me to go and apply because I would then be able to make my own money. I was hired as a dishwasher and was bringing home $17 a week. It wasn't a lot of money, but at least I was able to go and buy whatever I wanted without having to ask my parents. I only worked at St. Josephs in the wintertime during the offseason between soccer and baseball seasons of my junior and senior year. It was not only a great decision for me to go and work because I needed the money, but it also got me out of the house and away from all the craziness that was going on.

One of the best things that ever happened to me was meeting Kathy who was one of my classmates in Spanish class. I still remember the first time I saw her back in 1974. She sat directly in front of me. She had long strawberry colored hair and a great smile. Kathy was a junior, I was a senior. I remember saying to myself *"man, she is so beautiful"*. But I was kind of a shy kid back then and never really knew how to even approach a girl, let alone ask her to be my girlfriend. I had some friends who were having a keg party one day and had invited Kathy and a few of her friends to come over. Although we were in class together, it was at that party that we had officially met. We all had such a great time that day. Kathy and I exchanged numbers and would spend many hours talking on the phone. Things were going so great between us that I was invited over to her house to meet her father, Earl, and her mom, Peg. Earl and his brother owned a car repair business called *Bradley Brothers* and Peg was the librarian at our school. Kathy had two older brothers named, Paul and Mark who were both great guys, but they had already moved out on their own by the time I came into the picture.

Kathy was pretty much the main reason why I chose to stay at Elmira Southside High School. She came into my life when my family structure became broken and unfixable. She helped me survive my trials and tribulations associated with those family distractions. After all, she knew the dynamics of my family. When they say God will always send you an Angel for the journey of your life, Kathy became mine. Once we got together, we were inseparable. I guess you can say our relationship was worth walking all those miles back and forth to school. I remember when I used to try to butter up Kathy's mother Peg by bringing her some cookies, pieces of cake and pie from my home economics class I was enrolled in which happened to be near the school library where Peg was working at. Kathy's parents were always so great to me. They were totally the opposite of the parents who raised me. I spent a lot of time over at their house. They would provide me with home cooked meals, showed me that they loved and cared about me, and when it was time for me to leave, they would either give me a ride or hand me some money to call a taxi so I could get back home. Words can't express how much I appreciated all they did for me. Although I had some friends who had great parents who also treated me well, Earl and Peg were the perfect examples of what being real parents meant. Although they have since joined each other at the gates of heaven, I always hold them dearly in my thoughts and in my heart. They were just wonderful human beings.

Kathy was raised in the Catholic faith where family values were all intact. The more I spent time with her, the more I learned the true definition of what love was. She had been raised the right way which was a big plus for me because through her, I was able to express my deepest thoughts and all the pain I had endured throughout my childhood to her as she began to guide me each step of the way. Being able to talk to her and her parents gave me an outlet, but at the same time, it helped me heal mentally through the good times that we all shared. Especially when it came to my graduation. I will never forget that day and everything that transpired. Graduation is usually one of the first and biggest accomplishments for a teenage kid. Second to that would probably be getting your driving license.

The date was June 21, 1975. It was supposed to be the greatest day of my life. Unfortunately, and as always, my parents were always present when it came to stealing the show. If it wasn't ruining my baseball games while I was playing, it would have been them fighting at family events or just ruining whatever fun we were all having. This time, there was no fight. The only fight going on was me trying to hold back my tears. Both of my parents had attended my graduation. Earl, Peg and Kathy were also there in attendance.

The graduation took place at Dunn Field which was the minor league ballpark for the Baltimore Orioles and the place where we played some of our high school baseball games. Dunn Field was a Single-A elite ballpark in our town at the time because professionals used to also come and play there. As a kid, I would go there and watch Earl Weaver coach and enjoyed watching players like Boog Powell, Jim Palmer, Dave McNally. A few years later, they changed affiliations from the Orioles to the Boston Red Sox which was my favorite team. I then got to see players like Wade Boggs, Mike Greeenwell, and Curt Schilling play there too. I had been a witness to many things that happened between those lines on the field, but nothing in this world could have predicted what I was about to experience next. After walking across the stage to receive my diploma, I remember thinking to myself, *"man, that was fast".* Not just the graduation, but also my four years in high school. That was something that I have always made sure to remind any of the athletes I later coached or taught as a teacher because even though most students hated getting up to go to school, it all goes by so quickly.

As I sat there and waited for the ceremony to be over, I remembered how excited everyone was. I was happy too. But the only difference between me and all of them was the pain and loneliness I felt afterwards. I felt as if I could never catch a break. That same day, as I stood there holding my diploma, both of my parents came over to congratulate me. After hugging me, my mom walks off one way, and my dad walks off in the opposite direction. My parents were done. That was the very same day they would walk away from each other for good. I was left standing there struggling with my emotions. As if I hadn't already gone through enough of a mental beating throughout my childhood, them splitting up on what was supposed to be such a memorable moment in my life really crushed me. Instead, it turned out to be the saddest for me to have to deal with. My heart just dropped. I knew I was on my own right after that. The two most important people that I loved the most were now going their own ways. I knew what the word divorce meant, but this was more like watching it in real time as it occurred right there in the parking lot of Dunn Field. I'm not sure if that moment was symbolic in a sense of trying to predict my future in any way at the time, but as I reflect to that moment, I guess you can say in some ways that it could have been.

As I was about to burst out crying, Kathy came over and gave me a big hug which helped me cope with the situation. Earl and Peg always had a way of making me feel better. They knew what I had been dealing with when it came to my parents. But once we all got in the car, I controlled myself as best as I could and we all headed back to their house. To be honest, I was going through it so bad that I don't even remember if any of my siblings had even shown up to my graduation. That is all the memories I have from that day. Although graduation meant that I had some real adult decisions to make in the near future, that situation had temporarily set me back a little further. For that moment, I felt I was caught between two worlds. I bet there aren't many kids who can say that ever happened to them at graduation.

THE JOURNEY

"What doesn't kill us makes us stronger."
- Friedrich Nietzsche

Life after graduation came at me very fast. Although I had already known my parents were going through their separation, it took for me to see them walking away from each other to make it real. By that time, my dad had already left us and was living in his own apartment on the other side of town. I'm not sure if he was feeling a certain way about the way things had turned out between him and my mother, but he did call me a couple of days after my graduation and wanted me to meet him at a restaurant called Snooky's to have a few beers and have a conversation. We weren't there very long. He wanted to let me know that he would still be there for me if I ever needed him for anything. He gave me the address to his apartment which was across the river at a place called Wards Hotel and after two or three beers, we gave each other a hug and parted ways. My parents had been through way too much to continue the path they had been on. My mother was a little more obvious with her lifestyle, but my dad was no saint either. I later found out he was out and about doing his own thing with other women too. My dad passed away in January of 2019. Although there were many negative things, I had to witness him go through while he was alive, there are also many great things I can say about him. He was a hard worker. I cherish the memories I have with him when he would take me with him to work at his side jobs and let me be his clean up guy. He was tough and ruled with an iron hand and would occasionally use the belt to put me in line if I wiggled out of his expectations, but he was fair for the most part. My dad was a boxer growing up. Although he wasn't a big guy, he won the sectionals back in 1946 and1947 in two different weight classes. He had quick hands. I remember him sparring me up a couple of times while trying to turn me into a tough kid. I could never understand why he was always slapping me and punching me so hard across the face while intoxicated. It was a little too much sometimes, but all I knew how to do was try to fight back.

Although I was hurt by their separation, I guess it was better for them to just leave each other alone and find a better way to live their lives. I was eighteen years old and had to go and figure things out for myself too. I continued living at my mother's house for a little less than a year after my graduation before making my own decision to go out and begin my own journey. After noticing that my mother was developing relationships with other men from the Legion and seeing that my sister Brenda had pretty much become the caretaker for my two youngest siblings, I knew then it was time for me to leave. I didn't have any time for that. It got to the point where all I ever wanted to do was just eat and leave because I really didn't know what any of those guys were capable of doing to me.

I was close to three weeks out of high school and still had no idea what I wanted to do with my life. All I knew was that staying at my mother's house was becoming more and more uncomfortable for me by the day. While most of my friends and classmates went off to college or into the military, I was still trying to figure out my plans. I thought about joining the Air Force because going into the military seemed like an easier choice than to go out and trying to get hired somewhere, but I gave job searching locally a shot before coming to that conclusion. After going out and applying at different places, I was called to do an interview at Hills Department Store which was for a position as a Housewares manager not too far from where I live. I was happy to hear that I had been hired and I started working right away. My duties there at the department store included anything from ordering products, to keeping track of the inventory, stocking shelves and making sure that my two day and night assistants did their jobs. At times, I would also step in and play other roles where I would help unload the trucks or go onto the floor if it became busy. A buddy of mine named Dale, who used to date my oldest sister Debbie while in high school, had his own apartment. While having a conversation with him, he asked if I wanted to move in with him and go half on the rent. I didn't even hesitate to tell him that I was interested in moving in. Dale was a very nice guy and was a few years older than I was. Today, he lives in Albany, NY and he and I have always stayed in contact with each other throughout all these years and have remained friends.

Moving in with Dale was a great opportunity for me to get a good start on my own personal life. Not only had I been dealing with all the distractions at my mother's house, my sister Debbie, who I was very close to, had already moved out before I did. I felt bad about leaving behind my younger siblings Brenda, Sheila and my little brother Marc who was only eight years old at the time because I knew they would all have to go through their own trials and tribulations. They had to try to find a way to survive what I had already gone through myself. Fortunately, they did. It wasn't until years later and they became adults that they shared many of those crazy stories with me. But moving out was a decision that I really had to make. I'm sure my father was aware of everything that was going on with my mother, but there was nothing anyone could do about it. All my dad ever did was work and go home. I don't believe he ever came around the house after he had left. I barely did either. Besides, I had Kathy in my life, and it was more stable for me to have moved in with Dale because I wasn't going to be bringing her around my mother's crazy situations. Kathy used to come by but never stayed the night. I lived with Dale for about 2 years before moving on and looking for a new place to live. I lived in a couple of apartments before finally finding a house on the Elmira Southside. It was a single house that I rented back in 1978.

About a year later, I was promoted and became the manager in the toy department. That was a fun job for me. I oversaw ordering all the toys, assembling the bicycles and swing sets and then putting them out on display. Everything was slowly beginning to fall into place, and I was feeling a lot better about life. I was smiling and having a lot more than I had been before. In the meantime, my relationship with Kathy was going great. On my days off I would spend a lot of time with her or be out playing in the men's softball and basketball leagues in the area. Although I felt I had the opportunity to pursue a baseball career, I didn't see it worthy. All I wanted to do at the time was to have fun and be happy. I played those two sports continuously to have fun and stay in shape. Aside from all that, I would also have some of my buddies come over to hangout and have a great time with them. Those were my routines back then. I felt that's how things were going to be for the rest of my life and became comfortable with that. I was living the dream and enjoying it as best as I could. I had no complaints. I had peace of mind, which was very important to me, and I no longer had to deal or put up with any of the negative family situations anymore.

In the beginning of 1979, after four years of working at Hills Department, Kathy and I started talking about getting married. Once that became part of our plans, I knew that I would have to go back to the drawing board and start looking for a better paying job. Kathy already had a good job working at Marine Midland Bank. But I knew that it would be a matter of time before we would decide to start our own family and I wanted to make sure we would be able to afford to provide for them as well. I became very excited for our plans and really wanted to do everything I could to make that happen. At the time, there was a lady named Marlene who was also working at the Hills Department Store. She was a manager in one of the women's clothing departments and one day, we were in the breakroom talking and I had brought up to her that Kathy and I were planning on getting married. I went on to tell her that I was eventually going to look for another job where I could make more money. After hearing me out, she says to me *"if you are interested in trying to make more money, I know of a warehouse where they are offering $5.20 an hour plus benefits, and I could help get you hired there"*. I know that sounds like minimum wage these days, but this was back in 1979. Marlene went on to explain that her husband was one of the foremen at a company named Flickingers which was a food distribution center, and they were hiring like crazy at the time. I knew that if she were to put in a good word for me to her husband that I would have a great chance at being hired. I was so excited that I went home later that day and told Kathy all about it. Although it meant there was going to be a lot more work for me to do compared to what I was doing at the toy department, that new position would be paying me two dollars more from what I was making. After talking to Kathy about it, we both agreed that it would be a great idea for me to apply. Marlene brought me an application the next day which I filled out and later brought over to the company to hand in myself and within a few days, I got the great news that I had been hired at Flickingers. I went and gave Hills Department Store my two weeks' notice and then went on to start my new job.

I fell in love with my new job instantly. After many of my friends had found out the place was still hiring, they all went and got a job there too. The company offered all types of benefits which included dental, vision, and medical. You just couldn't beat it. Teamsters' benefits were all one hundred percent medical coverage, and they would even give us good raises every six months. Another great thing was that the company had their own softball team in which many of us joined and played for. They also sponsored many family events where we were able to bring our family too. Flickingers was a big company that serviced most of the supermarkets in and around our area. And boy, you're talking about getting in shape? Let me tell you, there was nothing easy about any of it. I was hugging my arms around cases of food all day long that I would have to stack up on carts to then wheel them over to be loaded onto the trucks that were parked in the bay areas. It was most definitely a grind. What kept me motivated was the great money that I had been making and the friendships I developed.

When Kathy came into my life, I was still struggling to find my own identity. I was doing things I knew could get me in a lot of trouble, but it was a phase I had to go through. While Kathy and her parents were deep into religion, I was out trying to make a few dollars while nickel and diming it. I wasn't religious at the time though. In fact, growing up, there was a church called North Presbyterian right across the street from our house which was also a summer school. I loved going there because they had it set up where if you had perfect attendance you could go on a plane ride. I ended up getting perfect attendance and got to fly over our city but ended up getting sick even though I thought it was pretty cool. But that's really the only time I ever went to church. It really had nothing at all to do with religion though. From the day of graduation, I was out there running the streets trying to be a knucklehead. I was heading down the wrong path from the moment I had graduated. I was working at Flickingers and partying with all my friends, but I also wanted to make a few more dollars on the side. I remember meeting up with a couple of my buddies and deciding that we wanted to become drug dealers. I was acting like an unstructured teenager with no direction. Maybe I should have joined the Air Force where I would have had structure and discipline I was lacking. Kathy still had one more year of high school left, and I kept telling myself that if I couldn't find a job that I would most likely have to go and join the military. But in the meantime, selling drugs happens to come across to being one of my choices.

We ended up hooking up with a dealer who was going to buy a quarter pound of pot from us. I had told him that we could meet him at his house, but he insisted that we met him at the park instead. After the exchange, we decided to spark up a joint with him. Next thing you know the police were rushing in. Once the officers conducted their investigation and the dealer admitted that the quarter pound was his, they took him away in handcuffs. Me and my buddy also ended up getting arrested for having a few dime bags in our pockets, but we got out on a couple of hundred dollar's bail after spending nearly 5 hours in a cell downtown. None of that went on our record because it was such a minor offense. The dealer who had the quarter pound went to jail and began telling other inmates there that he was going to get us back once he was released from the Chemung County Jail. Although he was the one caught in possession, he then turned around and began accusing us for him being arrested. It was the scariest moment in my life. I really thought I was going to become this big-time drug dealer but that was really the end of my drug dealing days. My life was just out of control. But Kathy was truly my savior. Lord knows where I would be today had it not been for having her in my life.

Kathy and I got married later that year in the fall of 1979 and she moved in with me. We stayed living at the house I had been renting for about a year before we ended up buying her parents' house. By 1982, we had our first daughter Carrie and then two years later, our son Michael was born in 1984. Thank God for the benefits I had at the time I was working at Flickinger's because they covered all the medical bills for our children's birth. Words can't express how excited I was to go through my own journey as not just a husband, but also as a father. Kathy gave me the balance and mental stableness I had always needed in my life. Especially when it came to raising our children together. From day one, I had always known that I wanted better for my children and wanted to grow up in a happy home. Although I had physically moved on from my own experiences of living under my parents, it was now our opportunity to play our part as mother and father. Kathy came from a structured home while of course I came from a broken one. While she had always known what it felt like to be loved and cared for, I had grown up always wondering how those two things felt. There are many people who believe that how you are treated as a child sort of predicts how you will end up becoming as an adult. But I knew that there was no way that I would ever treat anyone how I hated to be treated. Kathy and I made a great team. We knew what we wanted for our children. And that's why we have been inseparable since the day we met.

While working there at Flickingers my schedule would often switch depending on the shipments and how many staff members would be needed to complete the job. The main shift I worked at was 11 at night to 7 in the morning. While everyone would be sleeping back at home, I would be at the warehouse busting my tail through the night. There were a few times I would sit around and wonder to myself, *"holy crap, is this what I'm going to be doing for the rest of my life?"* Although the job was very tough, I was just sucking it up and doing whatever I had to do to support my family. If there was one thing, I did learn from my father it was to be a hard worker. It seemed my dad worked every single day no matter how he was feeling. I don't know if it was because he just didn't want to stay home and had to put up with my mother or not, but it was rare to ever see him taking a day off. I was the same way, but my reason to go to work every day was to make as much money as I could to pay the bills and be able to take care of our family.

As we are going through our situations in life, it is very difficult to determine whether things are falling apart or if they are falling into place. While many of us do get used to our daily routines, it is very rare that any of us stop to think that life could also be very unpredictable. From one minute to the next, your life can go from what it is in present times to sending you on an entirely different path that you would have never envisioned or ever imagined you would have to go through. It's sort of like many of us who just hop into our cars and drive from one destination to the next without ever expecting anything out of the norm to ever occur. Or like bungee jumping off a cliff and trusting that accidents would never happen. When I had asked myself "if working at Flickingers was how things were going to be for the rest of my life", I had no idea that question would be answered in the manner in which it came. Because if there was ever a moment in my life that I could go back and reflect on, all I can say is that it happened when I had least expected it. They say everything in life happens for a reason. Of course, it takes having to go through certain situations for us to determine why they occurred, but I do have to say this, I would have never imagined how one of my worst experiences in life would end up becoming the turning point which drifted me on a journey I never envisioned. While many say certain things happen by accident, mine was literally just that.

One morning, I was helping one of my co-workers named Dick Hadlock finish up loading a truck that he had been assigned to. Dick was probably in his fifties or sixties back then; I was in my late twenties. While he would do one or two trucks a night, us young bucks were doing five to six. So, I figured why not go and help him out. I told Dick to go take a break for a few minutes and that I would help him load up his truck. I must have already loaded up about two carts and while I was heading onto the ramp to load another one, I could feel the cab underneath me being connected to the trailer by the driver of the truck and thought nothing of it. I even remember saying to myself *"it's ok, he's just backing up the truck"* which was normal for them to do. Well, this driver must have been in a hurry that day because for some reason or another, he decided to pull his truck out without coming to the back to make sure that everything was secured and safe for him to go. There I was left straddling between the truck and the bay trying to scream over to Dick to tell the driver to stop, but he couldn't hear me because it was just too loud inside the warehouse. If you saw me from a distance, it was as if I was doing a split between the back of the truck and the loading area. Suddenly, the driver kept going and before you knew it, the ramp released itself from the back of the truck. I lost my balance and just slammed straight down about four feet to the ground and landed on my back. The driver must have heard all the commotion going and got out of his truck to see what had just occurred. When he came around to the back, he saw that I was laying there grimacing in so much pain. He looked down at me and had the nerve to ask, *"what the hell happened, why are you laying on the ground?"* I remember being so upset and thinking to myself that if I could have gotten up that him and I would have gotten into a fight. I tried getting up quickly but realized that something was wrong with my back. It took me a while, but I laid there until the initial shock wore off and I was able to slowly stand back up.

I went home after my shift was over and told Kathy about what had occurred to me at work. I tried laying down to get some rest and when I woke up a few hours later, I realized I couldn't get myself off the bed. I was in so much pain and had a lot of numbness throughout my back. I went and saw a few doctors and they had come up with the conclusion that there was a possibility I would need to have back surgery. The doctors explained to me that I needed to get as much rest as possible and that there was no way I would be able to go back to work. I was bedridden for close to six months. I had always been the type to be highly active and energetic and was always moving around. But all that came to an end suddenly. Not only was I not able to go to work, but I also wasn't able to go and enjoy my time playing softball or basketball with my buddies anymore either. That period of time really sucked for me.

It was an entirely new experience because all I could really do was just go to the bathroom and then go right back to my bed. After going back and forth to see the doctor, he finally gave me an ultimatum. He told me that I could go back to the warehouse but that within six months to a year that I would probably be needing to have major back surgery which kind of scared me. Although my normal weight had been between 130 and 145 throughout high school, I was a little obese and weighed about 235 at that time. To try and get back in shape, I started to do some light workouts to see if I could regain some of the strength that I had lost because I really did not want to have surgery. I did manage to get myself in somewhat better shape than I had been the past couple of months and then found myself in a situation where I had a major decision to make. I came across the thought of going to college, but that would mean if I left Flickingers I would be losing out on all my benefits.

After being out for approximately six months, I had a conversation with my doctor and explained my situation to him. I told him that I wanted to give working at the warehouse another shot to see if I could pull it through or not. The doctor then gave me the release and I went back. Well, long story short, I quickly learned that wasn't going to happen. Before my injury had even occurred, I had noticed how rough some of those foremen there would treat us. They could really stick it to you if they really wanted to. But I had made up my mind to try and get back to work. My first day back, the foreman gave me a 2-thousand-piece order. You would have never thought I had just come back from a back injury by the way he was treating me. He must have either thought I had been faking my injury or could care less about it. That same day, I ended up blowing my back out and going right back to the doctor to let him know I was all done with working at the warehouse. It got to the point where I couldn't even walk. I went and put in a claim through the New York State Disability Act and was approved to collect for some time. While I was collecting, I had a stipulation where I had to actively go out and document my daily activities. In other words, they didn't want me to just be sitting at home collecting disability without at least trying to show that I wanted to find a job I could handle. So, I decided that I would go and walk to the library every day and try to come up with some type of plan for my future. I vividly remember going into the office of the counselor I had been assigned to from the office of disability and letting him know that I had decided to enroll at Corning Community College.

To be honest, I really had no idea where college was going to take me. I knew that I could further my education and that it may somehow lead me in the direction of being able to find a good paying job somewhere, but other than that, there were no other real plans that I had made at the time. All I knew was I had a wife and two small children to raise and that I had to somehow figure out my life. That was it. By this time, I was already 28 years old and although I felt I was still good at playing baseball, I was not going to try out for the college baseball team because that was not my agenda. However, this is the moment I was referring to when I said I had no idea whether my life had been falling apart or falling into place. One day, while I was on the campus, there was a place they called The Commons. It was a part of the college where students would go to sit and eat, read a book or do their homework. While sitting there, I happened to look across the table and saw that the *The Corning Leader,* which was the local newspaper, had been left there. I went over and picked it up to look at the help wanted ads because I had needed a job. As I scrolled through it, I saw *"JV BASEBALL COACH POSITION OPEN"* in bold caps. That really caught my attention. I went home and spoke to Kathy about it to let her know I was really interested in the position and that I was going to call the school district for more information regarding the opening. When I called, they confirmed that the position was still open, so I got in my car and headed over to Corning to pick up an application which I ended up filling out there at the office. Two days later, I got a phone call to let me know that I had been scheduled for an interview with Mr. Alan Mallanda, who was the Athletic Director, and Lou Condon, who was the varsity coach at the time. I went and had the interview and a couple of days later I received a phone call asking me if I wanted to accept the baseball position. I remember thinking to myself, *"well, it's money, it's a stipend, and it's baseball"*, so it couldn't be all that difficult.

There I was, going to college and now I was being hired to coach the JV team over at Corning West High School. At this time, I was still collecting disability from my back injury. Although I had played baseball my entire life, I really had no idea what it would take to be a coach and to lead a team. But it sure as hell beats working at a warehouse or going out and getting another back breaking job. I felt everything was beginning to line up perfectly for me. I mean, what were the chances that I got hurt over at Flickingers, decided to go to college and next thing you know, I was being hired as a JV coach? It felt like a blessing to me and there was no way I was not going to accept that position. While I had been out on disability, I had no medical insurance for my kids and had it not been for Mema and Papa, who ran their own daycare helping us out we wouldn't have been able to go out and take care of business on our end. I got the position in the winter of 1986 and was due to start the season in the spring of 1987. The varsity coach, Lou Condon told me that he would help me out with my practices because he knew I had no real experience at coaching. To make life easier for myself

COACH JOHN M. KNAPP

and Kathy, I transferred to Elmira College which was a four-year school in my hometown because I had received a scholarship for transferring to go there. It was a reciprocal program that went to any student who wanted to transfer to Elmira, but you had to enroll into the teaching program in which I had decided to. I was very excited that all these things were happening because I was beginning to wonder deeply just where the hell my life was heading. My thought process at the time was, I could get a four-year degree at Elmira College instead of just going after my associates at Corning Community College. Elmira College was only ten minutes from our house where I could ride my bike to and from, Kathy could take the kids to the daycare or over to Mema and Papa's and then drive herself to work. Life became much easier for us after I had picked up that newspaper and saw that JV position opening. Life just began to feel much better for me from that moment on. Everything seemed to be on the straight line being that it was all within minutes to our house.

I think back to the days when I was working at Flickingers and wonder if my back injury was the way things were supposed to play out in my life for it to switch in the direction that I was heading. Had it not been for the injury, I would have never chosen to go to college and try to figure out another avenue to take. Then the newspaper being right in front of me as if it was meant for it to be there for me to pick it up and look in the help wanted ads. Regardless of what it was, I was ready to take on that new journey. And not just the journey as a baseball coach, but also to pursue a teaching career as well. That year, before I was hired as the JV baseball coach, I had only brought home $700 the entire year while on disability and I didn't even have medical insurance for my children. It was a little scary, but we managed to make it through. Being hired as the JV baseball coach at Corning West was a blessing. I couldn't wait to begin coaching. Baseball season only lasted a couple of months from March to May, and I knew that once the season was over that I would need to go back out and find another job. In the meantime, I just wanted to get out there and do my best. I really had no real idea of what it was I was getting into, but I had Lou Condon by my side to teach me the ropes.

My first season as the coach at Corning West went well. It was most definitely a great experience being that it was my first shot at being a coach. In the beginning of the season, Coach Condon helped me through the tryout process to select the best players out of about thirty who came out for the team. For the first week, I was pretty much his assistant. Once I was able to select my seventeen players, I was ready to go out on my own to lead the team. I didn't have an assistant coach to help me out, but luckily for me, I had some really great players who made my job easy for me. They were not only great players, but also great listeners. One of the best lessons Coach Condon taught me was to always plan everything ahead. I didn't want to have any of my players just running around without having any idea of what was expected from them. I studied every player that I had and placed them where I felt they would be the most productive at. Of course, there were only nine positions out on the field that I had to fill, but for the remaining eight, I always made sure to keep them involved somehow. I never wanted to make them feel like they weren't part of the team just because they weren't starters. Each and every player on my team knew what their roles were during practice and also for our games. I would always set up mini stations where players would rotate through during practice so they could all develop their skills at different positions. Baseball is one of those types of sports where players could go from playing in the outfield one inning to being on the pitching mound the next. I always kept in the back of my mind that no matter how well we planned, we also had to have a backup plan in the case where something occurred out of the norm. My main goal was to always be as organized as possible while also having as much fun as we could.

Regardless of what other issues I may have been dealing with in my personal life, I always made sure to never show it in front of the players. I wanted them to always know that I was not just their coach, but that they were my priority for those hours they were with me. They never had any idea if I was backed up on my bills, had a load of homework to do, or even if I was struggling with anything personal back at home. They all knew I had a wife and two kids back at home, but I always did my best to separate and tune those things out so that I could give them my full attention. Being that we were playing in upstate New York, and it was still cold outside in the beginning of the season, we started off by practicing inside the school gym. It was a little tough at first because of course we weren't out there on the field, but I was able to take it one step at a time and came up with some ideas to make it work. Once the temperature went up to about forty degrees, we were finally able to go and practice outside. I always made sure that all the players wore long sleeve shirts so they could stay warm. I had a lot of easy rules for them to follow. And whether they liked me or not, I never really looked at that as anything too important for me to worry about. I always showed them that I cared and loved them and if I had to be strict, they all understood that none of it was personal in any way.

As the season started, I always made sure to have team meetings before and after practice so everyone would know what the game plans were. One of the most important positions I felt I had to really be on top of was our pitching. I wanted my pitchers to have knowledge of when they were going to be on the mound a couple of days prior to our games so they could mentally prepare for it. Although everyone had an idea who my starters were, I also made sure I took care of my role players. As the coach, I always felt like I had to mix things up. Although my role players weren't just as good as my starters, they were also very important to me. I always looked for situations where they could be successful. There was nothing routine about what I tried to do. I always had to try to figure out the perfect lineup for that day in order to give us the best chances to win. And even though we were trying to win, I was always looking up and down my bench to see how I can use any of my players in key roles. Everyone was good in different situations. Some hit better than others, some ran faster, and some were just great players who I knew would make the game fun for us to enjoy. The only downside to having some of those role players was when they would complain about not starting over another player or when they would come to me and mention something that their parents would say about me and the way I coached. It was a challenge at times, but I always told myself that I was the coach, and I oversaw making all the decisions on the field. But for the most part, my players always went home with a positive attitude and always looking forward to the next game.

Being a baseball player myself, I had always wanted to make sure that I knew what my role was for each practice and for every game. So, I always made sure that my players knew theirs. Before every game, I always posted a lineup card where it included my role players, so they would know what was expected from them if and when the time came. I made sure to have them pay attention at all times, so they knew what was going on in the case where their name was called, and they had to pick up where we were at during the game. You just never knew what was going to happen out there. One minute everything could be going smoothly and next thing you knew, a role player would have to come off the bench to replace someone who might have sprained their ankle while sliding into a base. Then there were times when we were tied or down a run in the bottom of the seventh inning and needed to put some speed on the bases to try and win the game. As a coach I always had to go with my gut feeling and make the best possible decision for the team to win. As difficult as it would be sometimes, that meant that I would even take out one of my starting players who might have gone *0 for 3* and I felt one of my role players could go up there and give us a better shot at winning. When it worked, you were a genius, but when it didn't, there was always a chance you would hear it from the crowd. I will never forget Nikko Foti, he was a freshman player and brought up to the varsity team. We came across a situation where we needed a pinch runner. I had put him on first base and there was a ball hit in the gap and he ended up scoring all the way from first base against our rival team. The next day, you would have thought he was the king of the school after they had announced that he had scored the winning run. He was my fastest player on the bench, and I took the opportunity to use him in a situation where I knew he would give us a great chance. Today, Nikko is in the medical field as a professional., how about that? To this day, no matter what he does in life, he can always tell that story.

To me, it was always a gratifying moment anytime I would watch a player who had been sitting on the bench all game coming through for us. I had always reminded my players to *play the game, not the name.* In other words, I wanted them to focus more on playing how they normally would regardless of how good the other team was. It was always important for me to remind them of that because it would take off a lot of the pressure some of them would put on themselves. But for the most part, they were such good players that they knew exactly what to do each and every time they stepped foot out on the field. My first coaching season was a success as we finished the season with a record over five hundred and I began to learn how to build relationships with student /athletes. The second year of coaching the team finished the season 19-2. I still remember those two losses to this day. One of them was a thirteen/fourteen inning game against a team from Hornell, New York. That game ended on a very close call at the plate on a pass ball where they scored the winning run. It was a crushing loss. One of my players, who was also a football player, was so mad at the call that he wanted to get off the bus to go and fight a group of kids who were out there making fun of us. Our other loss was to Horsehead High School where we also lost by just one run.

I must admit, I might have played a role as being the coach, but we had such a great group of players that were placed in the right positions and did their jobs. It was really such a great experience and neat profession for me. We had so much fun that year and I remember telling myself that I wanted to keep coaching forever, but I never knew what my future was going to be at the time. Our last game, I walked off the field crying. It was very emotional for me. From a distance it just may seem like players running around in a uniform having fun, but to me, it was like my family away from home. I loved every student and player dearly. I can't express through words how each one of those players made me feel throughout the year. I went from searching for a job to make a little money to support my family to ending up having one of the greatest years of my life. So much so that I felt it would have never ended. We ended up with a great record, but that wasn't as important to me as the bond we had all created as a team. It became even tougher when the time came for all the players to turn in their uniforms. I was so emotional I cried the entire thirty-minute ride home.

When the season was over, I went back to the newspaper ads to the help wanted section and noticed that they were hiring at the Elmira Glove House group home facility which provided intervention for teenage juveniles who were placed in the facility's care by the Chemung County Family Court System. There were about five different facilities in the area. It was summertime and I needed a job. So, I went over and applied and got the job as a Childcare worker. In the meantime, I continued taking summer classes at Elmira College while in pursuit of my bachelor's degree. I would work over at the juvenile facility all year until baseball season started and would have my schedule switch to work doubles on the weekends. On top of that, I had to play the husband and father role at home. I would sometimes leave my house at 9 o'clock at night, head over to the college until midnight, come home and Kathy would catch me with all my books with arms stretched out across the table sleeping. I would be exhausted, but I knew that all my hard work would eventually pay off one day. By this time, my parents had both gotten remarried and we would occasionally meet up for holiday gatherings and have a great time. There was no longer any yelling or screaming like old times. They both kind of grew up and I was able to finally see the two of them just getting along. They were two great people who just weren't meant for each other. Things were finally becoming somewhat calmer in my life.

I went on to coach at Corning West high School for two season, and unfortunately that coaching position came to an end for me. There was a certified teacher who came in and had signed up to coach baseball the next year. Legally, in the State of New York, if you are a certified teacher and applied for an extracurricular stipend, whether you had any coaching experience or not, the school had to give it to them over a non-certified teacher. The Athletic Director, Mr. Mallanda, who was the one that had initially hired me for the Corning West JV position, came to me and explained to me that it had nothing at all to do with my performance, but that he had to follow the rules and offer the position to the new coach. However, Mr. Mallanda then tells me that there was another JV position opening over at Corning East and asked me if I would be interested in interviewing for it. I told him that I was absolutely very interested in the position and that I will go and apply. It was a very sad situation for me and my former players. It was tough for me to have to leave behind the great players I had been coaching, but there was nothing I could do about the situation. A couple of days after they had been given the sad news, I remember my wife Kathy calling me while I was working at Elmira Glove House and telling me that my players were all in front of our house. I told her to go and order them some pizzas and that my shift was ending in about an hour so I would be home soon. I had never seen fourteen- and fifteen-year-old kids cry before until that day. They were upset because I was no longer going to be their baseball coach. Seeing those players so upset that day became my *"aha moment"* because that's when I felt I had found my passion.

Mentally, I had put myself in their shoes and asked myself if I would have ever gone as far as they did to show my JV coach the love that they were showing me? Absolutely not. I hadn't realized just how much of an impact I had made in those players' lives until Kathy explained it to me. It was even crazier because they came back again the following weekend and told me *"Coach, we got something for you"*. And *"oh my goodness"*, I couldn't believe what they had done. As they all stood in my living room, one of them said *"coach, if you can't wear this jersey, no one's gonna wear it"*. When I looked over, one of them was standing there holding up my jersey. I couldn't believe it. They had broken into the equipment room where all the uniforms were and stole my jersey. I will never forget them or those two moments. It was hard for me to think of it in the way that I think today, but I had to keep it moving in life. The fortunate part for me was that there was a JV position opening over at Corning East which happened to be our rival at the time. I knew that my former players were probably going to be a little upset about it, but I had to do what was best for me and my family. It was a tough decision to make, but it was baseball. I jumped on it right away. There were a few other candidates, but none of them were certified teachers which gave me a better chance at getting the job. I had my interview with Mr. Mallanda and sat in with Varsity Coach Bill Thomas. I had a great interview and ended up being hired as the new JV coach over at Corning East. I didn't know it at the time, but I ended up becoming close friends and working alongside Coach Thomas for the next 14 years.

ALL IN WHO YOU KNOW

*"Everything will be ok in the end. If it's not ok, it's not the end" - **John Lennon***

After working my way up, the ranks at Elmira Glove House, I had been promoted to work under a program called Own-Home Supervision. It was a program where the juvenile client was remanded by the family court to Own Home Supervision Program where their behavior was being monitored daily at home or at school. Sort of like when an adult is paroled to their sponsor's home. I had a caseload of about 8 /10 clients who were adjudicated by the state of New York, and I could check on them whenever I felt I had to make sure they were doing what they were supposed to be. For the most part, the juveniles would behave because they didn't want to end up getting violated and be sent back to finish their time at a juvenile facility. I could check on them at school or show up unannounced to their home to make sure they were staying out of trouble. While at the position as a case manager, I was working closely with many of the probation officers and the family court judge where we would all meet up every Thursday to review all the client files to determine their placement. Once again, I came across yet another decision I had to make. One of the probation officers had put in their notice because he decided to go to law school which meant there was going to be a new juvenile probation officer position opening soon. For some reason, all the probation officers gathered and thought that I would be the perfect candidate to take over the position. There were two probation officers who came over to my office at Elmira Glove House and shut the door. I had no idea what was going on. They both mentioned to me that there was going to be a new position opening and that they had just had a meeting with a couple of other probation officers in the juvenile department and my name had been brought up. I thought to myself, well, the position had a lot better benefits, it was better pay, and maybe I don't have to coach baseball anymore. I was ecstatic. I went home and told Kathy all about it. After discussing it with her, I decided, *"why not give it a shot"*. I went and applied and was hired and after going through a three-week training at New York State Correctional Academy in Albany, I was then sworn in as a juvenile probation officer in Chemung County.

I was a man who wore many hats. One minute I was home being a husband and a dad. For the next eight hours, I was a case worker at the group home where I needed to focus because there was just no telling what I was walking into. After getting home from work, I had college homework to do. When I was done with that, I would go and paint a room or fix a leaky faucet because we couldn't really afford to hire anyone to do those jobs for us. Then, I would have to go and clean myself up to then must go and put my kids to sleep. I always had to prioritize when it came to my tasks. It never mattered how early I had to get up or how late I had to stay up, I always found the time to get things done no matter what. That was just the grind I had to go through to follow my path. There were times I wished we could have done more as a family, but we really didn't have the money to go on any vacations. For fun, we always made sure to go out locally to some of the parks and have picnics and do other small things with our kids to entertain them. They were small at the time, so they always seemed to enjoy the things we all went out and did as a family. I never viewed anything in my life as a burden or any of it being stressful. I just looked at everything as it being my responsibility in life to handle situations in the best ways that I could. There was a lot of routine, structure and adrenaline going all at once for me. And that's just how I handle it all.

I worked at Elmira Glove House from 1986 to 1990 as a case worker before becoming a probation officer in 1990. I did that for two years. However, I did stay employed with Elmira Glove House up until 1994 working as a Summer Rec Worker where I would take the juveniles out for activities like fishing, hiking, swimming, or to the local parks to have fun. When it came to being a probation officer, there were many similarities when it came to the conditions for the juveniles, except now I was in the position to make the decisions when it came to violating them. Plus, I already had the experience of working with the judges who handled juvenile cases, so it was an easy transition for me. Those two years were interesting to say the least. Like working at Elmira Glove House, I never knew what to expect as a probation officer either. Like the time I decided to go and watch a basketball game between Elmira Notre Dame against Elmira Southside who were rivals and were just a few minutes away from each other. I had two buddies who had sons who were on the basketball team, so I wanted to go and check them out. The gym was packed that night. There must have been at least a five hundred fans there that night. As I'm sitting there watching the game, I saw two juveniles who were on probation and had warrants out for their arrest walking in to the gymnasium to watch the game. Along with them were about ten other kids. They didn't see me and probably would not have recognized me anyway because I wasn't wearing my suit and tie.

At that time, we didn't have cell phones, so what I did was I went over to the two deputies and explained the situation to them. We went into a small office and figured out a plan on how we were going to approach the matter. I used the office phone to call my fellow probation officer named Jim to let him know about the situation as well. Jim went and called the judge to pick up the warrants. Before leaving the office, I also made sure to call Kathy to let her know that I might not be coming home right away due to what was going on. After coming up with the plan, I went and got a bag of popcorn then headed back to the gym to continue watching the game. Jim finally showed up, so I went down to meet with him back in the office along with the deputies. By that time, the deputies had already called for backup to assist them. We waited until the game was over and allowed most of the fans to leave the gym before making any moves. As soon as the two juveniles went through the exit doors, the deputies immediately grabbed them and brought them into the office. We didn't really want to cause a frenzy, so we allowed as much of the crowd to leave first. Once they had been situated in the office, Jim and I then walked in and presented the juveniles with their warrants. After explaining the situation to the juveniles, the deputies then went and placed them in handcuffs and began escorting them to their cruisers to bring them downtown to be processed. The rest of the posse they had come to the game with were all waiting outside waiting to see what was going on, so we made sure to keep an eye out for them too. As we were walking out, some of them began shouting at the deputies. One of the deputies turned around and told them that *"if any of you boys wanna go downtown with your buddies, stand right there and we can accommodate that for you"*. I was only supposed to be at that game for an hour or two as a regular civilian and didn't end up getting back home until almost midnight because I had to get back into probation officer mode.

Then, there was another time when I was two days removed from my MCL/ACL reconstruction on my left knee and had been placed on disability, but I had to testify in this big ongoing juvenile case where a juvenile was on trial for violating his probation numerous times. We had attempted many times to keep him out in the community, but he continued to violate his probation. I had to testify because the juvenile happened to be on my caseload. The situation with my knee was so bad that I couldn't drive myself down to the courthouse, so they had deputies come and pick me up at my house. But as difficult as the situation may have been for me at the time, I still had to put my suit on to attend the trial because I didn't want to disrespect the court and not look presentable. When I got there, there was a court attendant named Jackie who placed a chair in front of me so that my leg could be elevated and out straight. The juveniles' lawyer didn't care how much pain I was in though because he immediately began grilling me like I was the one trial who had done something wrong. But no matter how many tough questions the lawyer tried to throw my way I handled everything well. They wanted to make sure that I had tried everything I could to keep the juvenile from being violated and having to be sent to a higher-level care facility. I mean, this kid was no angel. Not only had he violated numerous times, one night he went and caused major damage to about ten cars he had jumped on that were parked along Pennsylvania Avenue in Elmira. Once the case was over, the juvenile had been remanded and sent to Hillside Detention Facility. The judge told me that I had done a great job and then told me to go home and get some rest. The juveniles' grandfather, who was there present at the courthouse, wasn't too happy with me. As we were leaving the courthouse, he began blaming me and even went on to threaten to kill me. Like his grandson, he too had been incarcerated a few times in the past for petty crimes. I really tried paying him no mind because I was just doing my job, but of course I knew to never take any of those threats lightly. There are many stories I remember from being a probation officer, but those are the two situations that always come to mind.

WHY ME?

*"Surround yourself with mirrors and watch the success grow" - **John M. Knapp***

They say that when one door closes, another one will open. It was becoming the story of my life. I'm not sure if it was luck or destiny, but to take a little credit for some of the things that were happening in my life, I worked very hard to get to where I am today. No matter what obstacles I had to deal with, I always found a way to overcome them. As I look back into my past, I remember the times when I would sit around and ask myself *"where is life trying to take me?"* Although I had been coaching baseball and had great work experience, I always felt motivated to continue to find what it was that truly made me happy. Things were going great at home with Kathy and the children and baseball coaching had become one of my favorite things to do, but I wasn't really settled on a profession just yet. I ended up obtaining my Bachelor of Science in Education and Athletics in 1990 while I was still working as a probation officer. In 1992, I came across a new 5th grade teaching position that opened in the Corning-Painted Post School District at one of the elementary schools in the area. Once again, I found myself in a situation where I had another decision to make. I had to decide whether I wanted to continue being a probation officer or to become an elementary school teacher. I was always up for a new challenge. Being a probation officer throughout the offseason worked out, but once the baseball season started, there were many times when I would find myself having to rush to my car and change from my probation officer suit and tie and into my baseball uniform.

After completing my second year of coaching at Corning West had gone on to interview for the Corning East JV position, I met a guy by the name Bill who was the varsity baseball coach at Corning East. Bill was also an 8th grade history teacher at a school named Northside Blodgett Middle School. Through conversation, I asked him to let me know if he ever heard of any teaching positions openings in the Corning Painted Post school district to please keep me in mind. Around that time, there was a situation at Northside Blodgett Middle School where they were planning to cancel the track season due to no one signing up to be the coach. When Bill heard that, he decided he was going to step in and take over the position because he didn't want the students to go without having a track season. Although he didn't really know anything about coaching track, he did know what it took to coach a team and sought out other people to assist him. One of the young girls on the track team who had ended up getting a scholarship was thinking about quitting to go play another sport because she had been told there wasn't going to be a coach. The girl's father, John Castiglione, who happened to be a principal at Calvin U. Smith Elementary contacted Bill and told him that if he ever needed a favor to let him know. The girl's dad was very grateful for what Bill had done. I had heard all my life that when it comes to moving up in the world that this is usually how some of these things happened. Although Bill stepping in as the track coach really had nothing to do with me, I ended up becoming that favor.

There was a 5th grade teaching position opening over at Calvin U. Smith Elementary where the young girl's father happened to be the principal at. By that time, I had already been coaching for 6 years in our district. Once Bill heard about the opening, he talked to the principal and told him that he knew someone who might be a great fit for the position. Out of all the possible candidates who had applied for the teaching position, I must have gotten skipped up to maybe five or six who were going to be interviewed. But here's a funny story leading up to my interview. A week prior, I had surgery on my ACL to have it reconstructed. I was still working as a probation officer at the time and being that I always had to wear a suit, I felt I was already properly dressed for the interview. My knee was killing me. but there was no way I was going to miss out on my new opportunity to become a teacher. I go and get into my station wagon and made my way towards the school. On my way there, I had to go through a town called Riverside. I looked up and noticed that the traffic was at a complete standstill due to construction. I started to panic and began sweating profusely because I really didn't want to be late. I looked at my watch and realized that if I didn't push it that I was going to be late. By the grace of God, I don't know why I never got arrested. I went over on the right-hand side and drove through the construction site. It felt like a movie. All the construction workers were trying to stop me, but there was no way I was going to stop. I had my mind made up that I was going to make it there one way or another. So, I just *stepped on it* until I was able to clear the traffic and make it through. I went and cut through a neighborhood and kept looking back to make sure there wasn't anyone trying to chase me down. There I was, a probation officer breaking the law speeding through a work zone. I didn't know if I was going to get my interview or end up getting arrested for driving like a maniac. I kept going until, finally, I made it to Calvin U. Smith Elementary. My heart was pounding, and I felt as if I was sweating through my suit. I walked into the school trying to act as if nothing had ever happened and the first person who I saw was the secretary, Joyce Everett. *"Hi, I'm John Knapp and I'm here for an interview with Mr. Castiglione.* I could tell by the way she was looking at me that she had noticed all the sweat dripping off me. She said to me *"it's ok, you can relax now, please have a seat, he will be here in about 15 minutes"* and then chuckled a little as she walked away because she probably thought I was sweating due to being nervous. She really had no idea.

Anyhow, I went through with the interview and a couple of days later I received a phone call where they had offered me the position as a 5th grade elementary school teacher. I had to make yet another decision as to whether I wanted to stay working as a probation officer or to accept the teaching job in a district in which I already had vested interest in my retirement through my coaching job. At the time, I really had no idea that I would ever become a teacher. After going over it with a few of the other probation officers and of course talking to Kathy about it, I weighed the pros and cons which for me was a no brainer to go into New York State Public Education because of all they had to offer including the state benefits which were a lot better than what the county could have offered me down the road. Although I had a great experience working as a probation officer, becoming a teacher was one of the best decisions I had ever made. I became a teacher at Calvin U. Smith Elementary and still had my position as a baseball coach at Corning East. When I was hired as the new 5th grade teacher, they asked me what I thought about the idea of some of the students who had special needs mainstreaming into my room for a little extra help and attention. My response was that all of us have special needs and sometimes needed a little more attention at one point or another in our lives and that's what we were all there for. Especially with me knowing of the past I had as a child. To me, if we had each other's backs to help the students become successful, I never saw any issues with trying our best to come up with the best solutions for them.

During my first two years of teaching, I was always trying to come up with different ideas to help all our students. Even though I was a 5th grade teacher, I was now having some of the 5th graders main streamed into my class for what we began to call multi-age class. Sarah Romans, who was a Special Ed teacher, and I had always wanted to invent a new program that was more energetic and more real for our students. We didn't just want to be hamsters in a wheel and do the same things day in and day out. Sarah, fourth grade teacher Donna Perry and I all got together and met with school principal, John Castiglione and expressed to him that we had this idea regarding the multi-age concept, and he told us that it seems like we were on to something and asked for us to continue working on it. After Sarah, Donna and I met a few times to go over our ideas, we then went back to Mr. Castiglione and presented him with the plan we had come up with where we would take the 4th and 5th graders who had special needs, along with regular ed students and move them to one area and have them rotate through by choosing from three different classrooms based on what was being taught each day. The students loved it. In fact, the district decided to come in and tear down some of the walls and put in sliding doors to make it easier for the students to go into different classrooms where they would learn from the different subjects each teacher was responsible for. This program was pretty powerful, and you could tell just by how the students were responding to it. We were all just so proud of our students. We were so excited that we even went to a seminar to present our program to others in Cincinnati, Ohio in front of over 500 hundred people. After our presentation, we saw a store nearby and decided to take a walk over to it. It was a stuffed animal store and we saw that they had one of a big cougar in the front as a display. We all agreed that we should purchase it and bring it back to our school for the students. Our school was named after Calvin U. Smith, so we decided to name the cougar Calvin.

Oftentimes, I would look at some of our students and it would motivate me to try harder each day to put a smile on their face and to make them happy. I knew what I had been through and understood how some situations could be back at home for them. But for the hours that they were with us, it was our job to make sure they stayed motivated and excited about coming back every day. Each month, we would rotate Calvin throughout the *Cougars Den* which was the name we had given to our classrooms. To keep the students happy, we would have Calvin sit next to them or have them comb his hair and even dress him up. The students loved Calvin. It never mattered what we were doing, Calvin was always involved in it somehow. But, by my sixth year at Calvin U. Smith Elementary Principal John Castiglione retired and a new principal was hired. I felt I needed a change in teaching positions.

Around this time, while having parent/teacher conferences *I* happened to run into a fellow teacher named Kevin who was a Lacrosse coach and a 6th grade teacher at Northside Blodgett. I went over to him and asked him if there were any openings over at Northside where he was teaching at. Coincidentally, he told me that there was going to be a position opening really soon. Once he told me that, I told him to please keep me in mind. I was back to square one and trying to find a place where I was happy working. Once again, I was back at the table talking to Kathy and explaining the situation to her regarding the new principal and her agendas and told her I was getting some vibes and that it might be time for me to find another teaching position. Even though it was going to be tough for me to leave the Cougar's Den, I knew a change in teaching position was in my best interest.

I was always the type to light up the room and make everyone happy. So instead of continuing to be looked at as the bad guy for voicing my opinion that it would be better for me to leave. I had also learned that when it comes to a job, you should choose happiness over money. I knew that I would not have any issues with finding another position because by that time, I had built a pretty good resume for myself. I had worked 4 years at Hills Department Store, 7 years at Flickingers, I was the JV baseball coach at Corning, I had worked as a case worker at Elmira Glove House, I had been a probation officer, I had worked as a 5th grade teacher at Calvin U. Smith Elementary and the fact that I had been working in our district for the past 6 years proved that I was really committed to working in the area. So that's what I did. Kevin ended up contacting me regarding the position at Northside Blodgett and I went over and applied for it. Just one year after I had left Calvin U. Smith Elementary to go teach over at Northside Blodgett, I heard that the Cougars Den folded. I ended up being a 6th grade teacher at Northside Blodgett from 2003 to 2009 before switching to become the school's Phys Ed teacher in 2010. While at Northside Blodgett, there were times when I would be asked to fill in for the principal whenever he had to go to a seminar across the country and there was even a time when I had to do it for 6 months while he was out recuperating after having back surgery. The superintendent did try to encourage me to go and get my administration degree to become a principal, but I didn't want to because once I become a principal, you wouldn't be able to continue coaching baseball in New York State due to it being two different unions. In 2014, I moved on to teach at the Corning-Painted Post Middle School for one more year and after 31 years, I finally retired from being a teacher and coach in 2015.

OFF THE FIELD

"Success is peace of mind, which is a direct result of self-satisfaction in knowing you did your best to become the best that you are capable of becoming."
- John Wooden

As I reflect on my 31 years of coaching, I truly feel that my life and the game of baseball pretty much ran parallel from each other. Baseball was really supposed to be my get away from all the personal situations we had going on in our lives, but I also had to keep in mind that off the field, some of our players were also facing similar situations I had gone through growing up. I could always tell when there was something wrong with any of them. I could tell from the way they looked and all the way up to when they took their first swing at practice. I knew my students and players personalities so well that I knew something was wrong with them from the moment they walked through the door. Whenever I came across a student who appeared to be having a rough time, I would always make sure to check on them to see if they needed a one-on-one conversation. That's pretty much what it was all about for me. It wasn't just all about winning or about making sure that my students did their homework every day. There was always more to it than that for me. There were many situations that I came across that reminded me of my own childhood.

During our season back in 1993, Kathy and I had received a phone call in the middle of the night from the mother of one of my players. My player, decided that he wanted to place what seemed was a suicide note on his bedroom door. His mother panicked because she had no idea what she would be walking into if she would have opened the door. She was hysterical when she called so I knew that it was a very serious situation she was dealing with. She asked for me to come over to their house to check and see if her son was ok. The player had been very depressed because his father had gotten into an accident a few years prior and had ended up in a wheelchair. Prior to the accident, his father used to be very active as he would take him out fishing, play catch and do many other activities that they would always enjoy. Once I got off the phone with his mother,

I went and threw on some clothes and headed over to see what was going on. It was a bout a twenty-five minute ride. I had no idea what I was going to be walking into. When I got to their house, the mother met me at the door. At the time, she didn't know what his conditions were behind that door. I went up and knocked on the player's bedroom door once and then walked right in. As soon as he saw me, he asked *"coach, what are you doing here?*

He was shocked to see that it was me standing there in his room. *"Hey, we gotta talk"*, I said to him. *"I'm here because Your mom called me because of the note you had placed on your door, and she told me that she didn't know if you were planning to try to commit suicide or to do some type of other harm to yourself"*. The player was maybe 15 years old at the time. I went on to explain to him that regardless of what he was dealing with, he should never put his mother in that mental state. We all shed a few tears, but we were able to get through with having a good conversation to where he even expressed to us that he would never do any harm to himself. On the way back home, I kept thinking to myself "why would they call me and not a family member or even the police?" But that was the type of relationship that I had with all my players and their parents from day one. They trusted me to the point where even if it was an off the field situation that I could come and fix it somehow.

I concluded that my life was making more and more sense to me as time went on. I had been through many of my own struggles in life. But now I was in a position where I could use some of my own experiences to make them better for every student and player I came across. The pervious player's struggled with not being able to spend the quality time he once was able to with his father once he became a paraplegic. He was used to being able to do many things with his dad. Although my own father was living with us and fully capable of taking me out to the park or to do other fun things, he and my mother were always too busy living their own lives. So, I understood his frustrations. I felt sorry for the player and I believe that's why I was able to get through to him by making him understand that we all go through struggles in life that we will always have to try our hardest to overcome.

Although it was always tough for us as adults to get younger children to understand that we have also been through many situations in our own lives growing up, I never gave up on them.

We might have had different struggles, but I knew they wanted to have the same things I also wanted as a child. And that was love and attention. He went through it, but he eventually came out of the darkness. The player went on to become one of the best pitchers in our league. He was the type of tough pitcher where he would throw inside not caring how the batters would feel about it. He didn't care if it was his own grandmother up in the batter's box, if he had to hit her, he would have. In a sense, I guess you can say he would take his frustrations out on the field which was much better than how he had been expressing himself. This was the first time I had ever dealt with a mental situation while being a coach. It sorts of brought me back to when I was a child, only as a coach I was able to help players get through some of their toughest times. I went from watching my parents acting crazy at my own games, to dealing with different types of behaviors that our juveniles displayed while I was a case worker and probation officer and now, I was facing similar situations with some of my baseball players. They might have not been as extreme as most of the juvenile cases I had to deal with, but it didn't take much for me to take in that some of these children just weren't loved as much as they deserved back at home.

I was the kind of coach who wanted to leave everything on the field once the game was over. Any mistakes I felt were made out there, we would discuss in practice or if it was something that needed to be discussed in private, I would pull the player into my office. The one thing I did not do was give any access to any of my players' parents to contact me anywhere off the field or at home when I was with my family. If I ever did encounter any type of situation where a parent somehow contacted me off the field, I would always instruct them to call the school and leave a message and that I would get back to them as soon as I could. The only exception was in the case of an emergency, like the previous incident used earlier in this chapter. Which did happen from time to time. But that players situation wasn't the first or the last that off the field situation I would come across. One of the worst emergencies I ever had to personally deal with occurred a year later in 1994. One of my players developed a severe and serious sinus infection and had been taken to the hospital by his parents. I remember this story as if it happened yesterday. In fact, I get the chills just talking about it. I was teaching in my fifth-grade class and remember the principal barging into my classroom. I could tell something was wrong judging by the look on his face. He says to me *"John, you have to get to Robert Packard Hospital immediately, one of your players is in bad shape, and they need you there"*. To go back a little bit about the player, his grandmother was the head custodian at our school and he would worked with her during the summertime. He was going to be our starting left fielder and bat in the lower end of the line-up during his sophomore year. I remember him coming to me and saying *"Coach, I can't wait for tryouts and to get our season started"*. He was very excited about the upcoming season. However, when the tryouts began, he didn't show up. When I noticed that he hadn't shown up for the second day of tryouts, I went and called the school nurse to check and see if she had heard anything about him. She told me that his mom had called the school and said that he had the flu and wasn't feeling well. By the time the third tryout came around, that's when the principal had come into my classroom to tell me that I had to stop what I was doing and rush over to go and see the player at the hospital.

The drive from the school I was teaching at was about a forty minute drive to the hospital where the player was. When I arrived, his mother grabbed me and started crying hysterically. When she told me what his last words were, I almost lost it. *"Please go tell Coach Knapp that I will be at practice. Please go talk to him"*. I couldn't believe that baseball was even on his mind given the situation he was dealing with. I then walked over to the doctor to check on the player's status and he told me that he was hooked up to respirators and he's passed away but his family wanted you here so you could say one last good-bye. I went into the room where the player was and saw that he was all covered up with bandages and all I could see was his eyes. I went over and hugged him and kissed him and then bawled my eyes out crying over him. He was already gone though. It was a very tough moment for me not just because the player was one of my baseball players, but because he was loved and was so young to have to go through that. He had been struggling with a sinus infection and his parents thought they could take care of it with over-the-counter medication. Unfortunately, the medication wasn't enough to heal him, and the sinus infection backed up into his brain and eventually died from it. He was just seventeen years old.

I was asked to do the eulogy at the players funeral and to be honest, that was probably the toughest situation I had ever had to deal with in my life. You never really understand in full when they say that no parent should ever have to bury their child until you are there to witness it for yourself. No parent should ever have to go through that. But the only way for me to cope with the situation was to come to terms that this was part of life. We are not in any control of it. I enjoyed the game of baseball and loved coaching my players. As time went on, coaching sort of got a little more difficult because as we all know, life goes on. Although I will never forget the player and what he meant to all of us, we all had to find a way to keep on striving. There was no way I could have ever prepared for a situation like that to occur while coaching. You just never expect anything tragic like that to ever occur. But just like they are thrown by pitches in a game, life can also throw you some unexpected curveballs.

GREAT MEMORIES

*"The dreams and passions stored within our hearts are powerful keys which can unlock a wealth of potential." - **John C. Maxwell***

Baseball players are corky and very superstitious. I myself never coached a game without Bazooka Joe bubble gum and sunflower seeds. During the games, I always kept my gum in my left pocket and the seeds in my right one. If we went on a two-game losing streak, I would switch it up. One of the reasons why I would always keep gum in my pockets was because there were children in the stands that would chase down and bring back foul balls. Once they brought the balls back to our dugout, I would hand them a piece of gum. There were times when the games would be so intense that I would chew gum and pop in some seeds at the same time. It was something that would always help me focus. It would jack me up because of all the salt and sugar, but it was something I felt I had to do to help me get through my games. In fact, there was a game where we had to play a league championship in a state-of-the-art baseball field. It was a brand new all turf park and they had a "no gum or seeds sign". Of course, they knew I was going to have a problem with that. I went over to Coach Gary Crook, who the field was built for and offered him a hundred bucks to allow me to chew my gum and spit out my seeds. While laughing at my offer he says to me *"just try and keep it to a minimum coach"*. There was no way I was going to go without my seeds or my gum. I was totally addicted to them. My addiction was so bad that I would order Bazooka Joe and my seeds by the cases and have them stacked in my office.

As I got older, chewing that gum really became a problem for me. I broke a molar in the 1995 State Championship game and ended up putting the gum right back in my mouth. I was so superstitious that I felt I had to keep that same piece of gum in my mouth. There were some players who thought they didn't need to be coached or told what to do because they were so good. Some of them made me so nervous because they wanted to go out and make decisions for themselves. I always reminded everyone that we were a team and that we had to follow the game plan in order to have a better chance to win. I never had any issues having to decide to take out any of my players if I felt I had to. But I always made sure to protect and fight for them when I felt they were right or had a good argument on a play. I'm probably the only coach in New York State that could probably ever say coached a team from the rooftop of a school back in 2006. We were playing against Horseheads High School which at the time was our rivalry. After 20 years of coaching, I had been thrown out of a game for the first time in my career. It was over a questionable call at second base. It was a hit at run play and our player swung and missed. Their catcher threw down to second base to try and catch our base runner stealing and I even saw clearly that their second baseman never tagged the runner. I wasn't really the type to ever argue with umpires, but this one was adamant. We were battling for first place at the time. I went out to let the umpire know that he had made the wrong call and he threw me out. I ended up having to coach the remainder of the game from out in left field. The rule was that if a coach or player had been ejected from the game that they would have to sit out the next game, which in this case meant I couldn't coach my team from the dugout.

We were scheduled to play next against Elmira Free Academy. I had a conversation with one of our schools custodian workers, and asked him if there was any way he could get me up to the roof at Corning East High School. That was around the time when Motorola flip phones were out. He says" sure, *I can get you up there coach*". He walked me over towards the ladder that led to the roof, and we were even able to set up a desk right behind the air ducts for the AC and no one will be able to see you. Prior to the game, I went and made up the lineup then turned it over to Coach George Bacalles who was my assistant coach. As the game went on and things got heated up, I would call Coach Bacalles to tell him who to warm up or who to replace out on the field. He executed the game very well, but we still ended up losing. After the game was over, I went over to the coaches of the other team who I had known very well and told them that although I wasn't present in the dugout that I had been coaching from the rooftop of the school. They laughed their asses off once I told them. That was a fun memory for me to be able to assist a game by phone.

There are also many other fun memories that I will never forget about. Like the time when my sophomore pitcher found out during practice that we were going to be playing against Manny Ramirez's son down at the IMG Academy in Bradenton Florida. He came over and told me that he was going to go down in history and purposely hit him as soon as he came up to bat. *"You're going to do what?"* I asked him. Sure enough, as soon as Manny's son stepped into the batter's box and got ready to hit, he plunked him on the leg. I couldn't believe he went out there and did that. I'm sure he remembers that story and has probably shared it with many people throughout his life. Although I didn't agree with what he had chosen to do, it is a memory that he will have forever. Taking my players on the road to play in different states was probably the most fun we always had as a team. Throughout my coaching journey, I have taken my teams to play in many tournaments outside of New York. We traveled to Myrtle Beach, South Carolina to participate in an annual baseball tournament. Also, we traveled to the state of Florida to play at the Cocoa Expo Baseball Facility in Cocoa Beach, and the IMG Academy in Bradenton where the team participated in the first annual IMG Academy Baseball Classic. It was a big responsibility taking them on the road, but it was all well worth it.

There were times when the parents would even drive them down and we would rent vans to get around in. I remember one time when we were just about an hour away from getting back to Corning. Our fifteen-hour trip turned into a seventeen-hour trip. We were near Williamsport Pennsylvania which is usually where I stopped on the way home to let the players go get snacks or to use the restroom. One of my players ended up getting sick in the bathroom while we were outside gassing up the van. Not thinking it was going to take long, I sent another one of my players to go in the bathroom to check on him to make sure he was alright. When I noticed he was taking a little too long to come back out, I went in there to check on him myself. We ended up being there for about an hour and a half because he was not only vomiting, but he also had a severe case of diarrhea. At the time, that was maybe our fifteenth year of taking trips in the school district vans to go and play. I thought to myself that there had to be an easier way than to have to drive that many hours with our players. I went over it with my coaching staff and parent association, and we all came up with a new plan. After that trip, we decided that we would fly down to Myrtle Beach and rent vans at the airport instead of driving all the way down from Corning which made life a hell of a lot easier for the coaches and I.

Another great memory that I will never forget was our version of the *"Bill Buckner"* play. This happened back in 1995 in the New York State semifinals against Marlboro High School where the opposing team's pitcher, Rob Bell, had never lost a high school game. His career record was 23-0. Not only did we have to face him that day, their very first batter, Dermal Brown hit a 400 feet laser shot to dead center and over the fence. I guarantee you that ball never went higher than 20 feet in the air. I looked over at Coach Thomas and said to him *"man, we're in trouble"*. Rob Bell, who was 6 '3 weighed about 220 pounds was the number one draft pick for the Atlanta Braves in 1995 and played for several other Major League teams throughout his 13-year career. Bell was mowing us down that game. The 7th inning started with one of our players, getting hit by a 90 mile an hour fastball. The player never flinched. He just threw the bat back towards the dugout and headed down to first base. Bell managed to get two outs after that, then our next batter singled. So now we had two runners on with two outs. Our next batter hit a dribbler down the first base line where all the first basemen had to do was field the ground ball and the game would have been over. For some unknown reason, that ball took a bad hop right next to the base and ended up going between his legs and into right field. Coach Thomas sent both of our runners and we ended up scoring and taking the lead. You could sense the tension in the other dugout because Bell had never been behind or beat in his high school career up to that moment. We ended up bringing in our best relief pitchers where he closed the game out for us, and we ended up handing Bell his first and only loss. That game energized us to go into our next game, which was played that very same day, against Levittown Division High School out of Long Island where we ended up beating them and winning the state championship that year.

There were also two other bad memories, one of them involving my shortstop, who had taken a bad hop while warming up for our game against city rival Corning West. The ball came up and it blew his mouth apart resulting his tooth to pop out and land on the dirt. After a brief search, I ended up finding the tooth wiggling around like a little worm because the nerve was still alive. We went and got some cold water to rinse it off then placed it right back into the hole in his mouth and packed it in a bag full of ice. The good part was that the player was transported to his dentist to have surgery where they were able to save his tooth. The sad part was that he never played baseball again. The other incident, which also involved having a tooth knocked out occurred back when I was coaching the 7th grade girls modified basketball at Northside Blodgett where one of the players, smacked her face up against the bleachers while trying to chase down a loose ball causing her tooth to fall out. Like the other tooth incident, there was blood pouring out all over the place. The 8th grade coach, wanted nothing to do with it due to how gruesome it was. I sent him down to the nurse's office to get some ice. She had found the tooth and had it in her hand. I took the tooth from her hand rinsed it off and put it right back in her mouth. Only problem was, *I had put it in backwards.* After realizing what I had just done, I said to her, *Coach Knapp has to just make one adjustment and we should be good".* I quickly pulled the tooth back down, twisted it and shoved it back in place. It was a little painful for her, but we went and put an ice pack on her face and off she went with her father to the dentist to have it sutured back together. In baseball terms I was two for two in tooth repair and batting 1000!

THIRTY-ONE YEARS

"Success is easy if you believe" **- Zig Ziglar**

When I began coaching back in 1987, I really had no idea what I was getting myself into. I knew what it was like to be a baseball player, but leading a team was all new to me. What was a desperate move on my part to try and find a job to support my family became a journey that I will cherish forever. But I truly believe that everything in life happens for a reason. I wonder sometimes what my life would have been like had I not been hired to coach baseball. Prior to picking up that newspaper in The Commons lounge, my life was headed in a totally different direction. Although I really didn't have a gameplan when I had been hired, what mattered most to me at the time was that I was no longer going to be working at a warehouse anymore.

I ended up coaching JV baseball for 11 years before taking over the varsity team at Corning East after Coach Bill Thomas retired in 1998. At the time, none of us had any idea that Corning East High School located in Corning N.Y. and Corning West High School located in Painted Post N.Y. would be merging sports programs in 2010. It was tough due to the two schools having been rivals for over 40 years. It tore up the community because they all had voted against the merging of the high schools and middle schools. However, the superintendent did have the ability to merge the sports programs between both schools. There was a lot of animosity, and I knew that most of the parents were probably thinking that I was going to favor the Corning East side being that I had been coaching them, but that wasn't the case at all.

Once we had all come to terms that our sports programs had merged, the community was given another proposal with the state aid and the vote on the capital project went through to merge the schools. Construction for the project began immediately and coaching positions were posted. I applied along with the head baseball coach at Corning West. After a long interview process, I received the position despite the fact that the other coach was a Division 1 player and former first round pick in the Major League draft. I was extremely excited to have won the position over him. To ease the transition, I coached the summer Corning Legion team to try and help in establishing the relationships with most of the players and their families. There were quite a few challenging incidents that I had to deal with, but overall, the transition into merging the teams went well. I felt that would be the best option for me to help ease the tension and to make the transition between both sides. I knew it was going to be an intense situation for the players and the parents, but regardless of how much input they wanted to have, I had to make it so that everyone understood I was the one in charge of making all the decisions. It worked for the most part, but I knew that I wasn't going to be able to please everyone.

The most difficult part for me was to decide which players made the team and who I was going to have to cut. One of the hardest cuts for me to make was when it came to one of my Corning East players. His father was the chief of police in Corning. I had even written the player a letter of recommendation for West Point, but when it came to trying out for our team, I had to cut him. That was tough for me because when he played for me before the merge, I had a role for him. But there was nowhere that I could place him on the team. It was so tough that I even cried on my way home from the school because of how bad I felt that I had to make that decision. I was very emotional. The coaches and I tried everything in our power to try and figure out a way to keep him on the team but in the end, we had to come to terms that he just wasn't going to make the team. There was not only a limit as to how many players I could have on the team, but we also only had so many uniforms to hand out. In fact, none of the coaching staff wore a uniform so that we could have it available to some of the players. The coaches wore baseball pants and a pull over shirt that said Corning Hawks on it. In the end, I didn't even know how many Corning East players and how many Corning West players made the team. All I knew was that we chose the players we felt gave us the best opportunity to win and that was it.

Trying to decide what our team logo was going to be on the baseball hat also became a difficult task. I couldn't put an E on the front of the hat because we were no longer Corning East. I couldn't put a W on it because we weren't Corning West either. I even tried to intertwine the names between the two schools, but still couldn't come up with the design for the baseball hat. The school district sports programs mascot would be a Hawk so

I made the decision to put a Hawk on the baseball hat as our logo and that's what we stuck with. I wanted to make both sides happy and not have the parents be upset if I had chosen a name solely based on Corning East because I knew that wouldn't be fair. After that, every team including the basketball and football teams became Corning Hawks in the end.

There were many times where I found myself having to constantly switch hats and go from being a coach one day, to being a counselor and even stepping in as a parent to some of my baseball players. Baseball played just a small part in the bond that we all created as a team. Yes, of course we wanted to win as many games as we could. But to me there was always a lot more to it than just winning games or getting to the championship. It was a combination of the many things I had learned about the game throughout my years of playing the sport and all the way until I ended my coaching career. Sports to me was like being part of an extended family away from home. It sort of gives people the opportunity to escape the seriousness of life or the many situations we sometimes feel get the best of us. It's a break from all of that. But even through all of that, there were always going to be many obstacles that we had to deal with also. The players were always great. When the school district decided to combine the two schools' sports programs, I decided to help ease the transition. I would coach the summer legion program that consisted of players from both high schools.

Again, not because of the players, but because of how some of the parents and their analogies made it difficult for me to get everyone on board as one team. As a coach, you're sort of stuck between the parents being behind you in the stands and the players on the field. If any of you have ever coached any types of sport, you would know just how I felt sometimes. When you're on top and winning, you were the greatest coach on earth, but when you were losing or the parents felt you made the wrong decision, forget about it, they became ruthless. And I understood all that. I was a player once and had to deal with my parents screaming and hollering when I played. But again, it was, and it will forever be just a game.

My goal has always been to be a mentor to all my players and to love and build a great relationship with them. When it came to the parents, I always did my best to encourage them to just sit in the stands and enjoy the game because it was going to be short lived, and their children were going to be walking across that stage at graduation and moving on to bigger and better things in life. I felt the last memories they should be building with their son was to make a great one where they all would remember them as parents sitting in the stands cheering them on instead of embarrassing them. Throughout my coaching career, I had so many great students/athletes who I still think about today. They have no idea of how much they helped me get through some of my own personal struggles. Many people look at the game of baseball and may consider it to just being a sport. But I always viewed it a lot differently compared to how others would describe it. Throughout my journey, I've coached well over five hundred student/athletes and I still remain in contact with a few of them today. If someone were to ask me what my record was in all the years, I coached I would have no idea what it was. I know for a fact I won more than I lost, but that is all irrelevant to me. Of course, the wins were great. But we had a lot of fun and learned many valuable lessons with the losses too. I not only coached because I loved and enjoyed the game of baseball, but it was also the great relationships that I built with my players and the love I had for the program. It was never about Coach John Knapp. Even when we won big games, and the newspaper would come over and interview me I would always send to the player who went two-for-three and drove in the winning run or over to the pitcher who pitched a complete game shutout. I always kept in mind that I was never the reason why we won the games because they were the ones who had to go out there and play hard, not me.

I quickly learned that there was more to coaching players than just their athletics and academics. There were many times where I had to put myself in the shoes of some of my players, but luckily for me, I was able to fully understand most of their issues having gone through them myself as a young teen. One of the most important responsibilities for me was to listen to them. I allowed them to talk about their problems because in most cases, all they really want is to be heard. Although we were all out there to play and have fun, I always had to keep in mind that they also had a life outside of baseball. I truly believe that playing sports can save the lives of many kids or at least limit them from getting into a lot of trouble. One of my biggest fears as a coach was when the season ended, and I was not there to protect my players. There were a few players that I worried more about than others because I knew that once the games were over, they wouldn't have the structure that they had during the season.

I was always the type of coach who would put my arm around the players and tell them that it was ok when they struck out or made errors on the field. During my meeting with the players, there were some issues that would come up. At my parents' meetings, I would often remind the parents that their sons weren't going out on the baseball field to purposely strike out or make an error because ironically those plays are part of the game. I would encourage them to go turn on their televisions and go watch a major league baseball game and they would see million-dollar athletes making those same mistakes also. As much as they didn't want to hear me say it, I always had to help them remember that it was just a game.

Building the fundamentals was always a big priority for me. Not just on the field, but also throughout life. I always reminded them to do the basics and to try and keep fundamentals as basic as possible. Another priority that was also very important to me was that relationship that I would have with all my players. It was never a matter of whether they liked me or not, it was always about the message I tried to instill in them. I felt I had to know my players as best as I possibly could in order to be able to deal with each different personality I came across. No player was ever the same. All of them came with not only their own personalities, but also their own issues I had to sometimes step in and help them through.

Yes, baseball is the game, but it was always the lessons that baseball taught that I always tried to instill in my players. One of the best inventions ever created for me was social media because of how much feedback and content I receive from former players. Before Facebook or any source of social media, once a player graduated, I wouldn't hear from them unless they came back to the school to visit. Things are much different today. It's great that we can all stay in touch and see the progress most of the student/athletes have made throughout the years after they graduated. No matter where they are or what they are doing, it is a blessing to me that we can reach out to one another at any time. Knowing that they can still reach out to me for advice or just to have a conversation to catch up on things is a blessing. I know how tough life can get after graduation. Once you're no longer waking up each morning and hanging out with all your friends or teammates on the playing field, life happens. You must get up and go to work, you have bills, and you may have kids and a family to support. Life sort of comes at you from all angles. As an adult, you have all the responsibilities your parents had when they were taking care of you. There's nothing easy about that. So, when I get a phone call or a message from any of my players. I am still able to help them in any way that I can. Coaching for me never ended just because a player moved on with his life. They are and will always be one of my players even when they become adults. It's a bond that's unbreakable. It doesn't matter if you were my star player or someone who came off the bench. I loved and cared for all of them equally.

As a coach, I was able to see many of the situations that were also happening off the field with my players and even their parents because I was able to read through most of their faces and knew when something was going on. You can tell by their mood swings, how they performed on the field or gave me shorter answers than usual. Yes, I was their coach. But when those types of situations came up, I had to switch it up to becoming a counselor or take on the role as their father for that moment in time. I always tried to be as transparent as I could be towards everyone in my baseball program. One of the most important lessons for me was to use some of my own situations in my personal life to allow them to understand that I wasn't perfect just because I ran the team. I was also in their shoes once.

I remember how embarrassing it was for me when my parents would come to my games, and they would end up getting thrown off the property over their crazy behavior. I can remember as far back as when I was just ten years old, and my mother being kicked out of my Little League game for yelling at the umpire over balls and strikes. Or the time when I was having a really great time playing shortstop at one of my Babe Ruth games when suddenly I see the police pulling up and me thinking to myself, *"man I hope this doesn't have anything to do with my dad"*. And sure enough, there he was being taken away and into a cruiser in handcuffs because he was so intoxicated and had gotten into a fight out in the left field area with my mother. I can't tell you how embarrassed I was that day. I never really knew what was happening off the field because I was so into my games. I didn't have to go through those embarrassing situations while I played in high school because they were either at work or were just too busy with their lifestyles. It was always some reason or excuse as to why they couldn't make it. There were times when they didn't even have an idea that I even had a game. They had no clue. Like the time we went into extra innings, and I came home late on that Friday night. It was my senior year, and we were playing against Elmira Free Academy at Dunn Field. The game ended up going up to 17 innings and when I walked into the house around 8:30, my father began questioning me because he thought I had been hanging out on the streets even though I was clearly still wearing my uniform. But I was sort of happy that they didn't come to any of my games because I was always afraid of them embarrassing me like they had in the past.

Through my own personal experiences, I have learned to coach some of the parents on how to behave while at their own son's games. I would always have to remind them that they represented their child, our school district and not to embarrass them like my parents did me. I could always see the parent's reactions anytime I would share some of my own experiences with them because they just couldn't believe that I had to go through that myself. Many times, by sharing my stories of how my own parents were would make them realize that they were overreacting and should never put themselves in a situation where they would be judged in the same way my parents were.

In 2018, I became the head baseball coach at Notre Dame High School, and the home field just happened to be the very same field where my dad had been arrested at my babe ruth game when I was 13 years old. . One day, after one of those games, I went and stood at the exact same spot where I had witnessed my dad being arrested and looking up and saying to myself *"man, there goes that vision again of me seeing my dad being taken away".* I sort of took it as a sign from God where he was placing me there to coach for a couple of years so that I would remember what it felt like being an athlete and having to deal with those types of situations so that I would be able to use it as a tool for whenever any of my players experienced similar situations. And for the most part, it worked. As much as I wished my childhood was different, I made sure to try and make all my athletes and students' lives as eventful as I possibly could. When it came to their parents, that was an entirely different situation.

There were many situations where I had to talk myself out of engaging in a conversation or before reacting because I know just how passionate some of them were or could become while watching their son play. This is an example of what I mean by that. There was this one softball game I was attending where my then ten-year-old granddaughter was playing in. There was a father of one of the other players standing right behind the backstop. He was standing about ten feet from where I was at. He starts yelling to his little daughter to *"move up on the batter's box"*. I mean he was so loud you could probably hear him way out in centerfield. His daughter looks back at him and she moves up like he had instructed her to do. Now mind you, she's just out there trying to learn the game and having fun. But it was her father back there, so she felt she had to listen to him. After she had moved up in the batter's box, he said to her *"no, you moved up too far, you have to move back"*. So, the little girl moved back as the pitch was coming in and she took a swing at the ball and missed. I have to admit, I was a little bothered by it, but I felt I had to stay in my lane. I didn't want to cause a scene at the ballpark like I had experienced as a player myself. So, after the girl takes her swing and misses, her dad yells *"why don't you keep your feet still"*.

I couldn't believe he would even blame her when he was the one distracting her. As much as I wanted to go over and talk to him, I knew that it probably would have caused a big problem. I was never a big fan of those types of parents because all they were doing was taking away their kids' focus from the game. In fact, I couldn't stand it. I mean, that's what they have coaches for, right? Those were the types of topics and situations we would have discussed at our parent meetings. I know parents want to see their kids be great and do whatever they have to do to win. But not only did I feel they should always allow their children to have fun and enjoy themselves, but to also not become a distraction while the game was being played. In fact, I never felt the game should be brought home either unless it was something positive being brought up. Because I also had to deal with players coming to me and asking me to go and talk to their parents because they were getting in trouble for the mistakes they were making on the field.

I'm not sure if it's because I'm looking at sports from the outside these days, but I truly feel that these incidents just aren't the same anymore these days when it comes to today's athletes. I sometimes feel players are being forced to play one sport where they are limited from showing their skills or participating in other games that they may enjoy. After a few seasons, they are mentally unmotivated, burned out, having surgery, or just don't want to play anymore. You can only run a thoroughbred so many times before they finally give up. That's what I see happening a lot these days. Students/athletes are overused physically and mentally. In fact there are several athletes who play a couple different sports at the same time all year around. There is just too much pressure coming from the parents and even some of the coaches to the point where it drives some of those athletes to wanting to quit. Sports are supposed to be fun. An athlete must love the game for themselves rather than to be forced to play. And when it comes to winning, losing and even making mistakes, we can't blame them or accuse them of not trying hard enough. That too can cause them to never want to play anymore.

I feel that there are so many crazy situations that are happening in youth leagues today that are just overwhelming and at times very concerning. There are many people who take sports seriously to the point where it has become dangerous. Not only have I witnessed so many of these types of incidents throughout my years of coaching that I had to step in and try to resolve, but there were also many times where I witnessed many situations where fights would occur and even some of the bats from the field being used to settle their disputes. Watching my father being taken away in handcuffs was bad enough for me, I can only imagine how some of the off the field situations were being handled at home when no one was around to see or hear it. As a coach, it was tough for me because any issues that my players were bringing onto the field could affect their performance. I couldn't stress it enough to the parents during our meeting that they needed to take a step back and allow us as coaches to make whatever decisions we needed to make to keep the players happy or comfortable enough to want to play. Especially when it came to my role players because I knew how bad they wanted to get in there and play.

There was a time when Kathy and I had just come back from vacationing down in Key West for about 10 days. We had an amazing time. I knew I had to get back because we were getting ready to start the season for our American Legion games. I came back feeling good and refreshed. While I was away, my coaching staff helped with the practices and getting the players ready and in shape. A couple of days after getting back from our vacation, I had to be at Mansfield University , Pennsylvania for a summer baseball tournament. I pulled up and talked and had a meeting with all the players and coaches to make sure everything was alright and then headed to the bathroom quick before we started the game. While in the bathroom right in front of the urinal, one of the players' grandfathers confronts me and says, *"what you did to my grandson was wrong"*. I couldn't believe it. There I was in the bathroom trying to pee and I couldn't even do that in peace. What happened was his grandson was failing academically even after school district intervention, his school attendance was very poor so the school district took away his athletic privilege until he showed school improvement. His grandfather wasn't too happy about it, but I ended up having to explain to him that I had to follow the school district athletic code of conduct and that it was not my policy. It was an uncomfortable situation for me to have been in but that was just an example of the types of cases I sometimes had to deal with.

Throughout time, I have learned that life is more like a movie where we're the actors who play in many different stories. One minute you're the star who shines bright and everyone loves you and the next minute, you're the villain or victim who ends up having to deal and suffer with the consequences. And no matter what the script is or how we felt it could have played out differently, God is not only the film maker, but also the producer who oversees all the endings. When he yells cut, that's it. You can go back and watch those movies you have collected in your memory bank, but the outcome and ending will always be the same. But he will always continue giving us many more opportunities to audition for many different roles throughout life until it all comes to an end. Regardless of the outcome, I reminded myself daily that I had to continue to reinvent myself and play a different character for whatever role I had to step into next. My job wasn't easy because it was very difficult for me to please everyone all at once. Not even winning a game made everyone happy because some would have found a reason to turn it into a debate on whether I should have called a different play or put their son in instead of another player. But one of the best values I had as a coach was make my players my priority and not their parents.

I often sat around and told many of my childhood stories to my baseball players to give them an idea of what my life was when I was their age. Many times, they would be left speechless or stunned that I had ever gone through any type of struggle in life because they couldn't picture any of it happening to me. There were also times where they would even laugh because they thought I was joking around with them. They really had no idea that I had been through many of the obstacles and challenges they were going through or even worse. But I always felt that it was my position to help them as best as I could with the situations they had to face. And not just them, but there were also many times I would have to sit down with their parents to assist them with figuring out better ways to deal with the situations they too were facing. I know that being a parent isn't easy and you always want to see your child become successful in life. But there are times when you must let them grow and go through situations on their own to try and figure things out for themselves.

FAREWELL

"Failure inspires winners. And failure defeats losers."
- Roger Kiyosaki

Being a coach for 31 years was very rewarding and satisfying. I never looked at it as a job. It was a passion and something that I really loved to do. It molded me to become a better person and it taught me how to deal with adversity and different personalities. I even learned many lessons from the struggles and the failures that came along with it. As we all know, it is very difficult to accept failure when it comes to situations in life. The gratification comes from the players who reach out to me and say things like *"Coach Knapp, we thank you for loving us and for always having been there when we needed you most"*.

I have always been the type to have an open-door policy when it came to all the students/athletes which was something that I continued doing while working as a athletic performance fitness coach. No matter what, I always had a minute for any youth that came to me because I knew how important it was to listen to them. To me, it never mattered whether it was a 5th grade student or a senior in high school who was coming into my classroom or office and needed to get something off their chest. I never gave them any excuse or told them to come back later even if I had over twenty papers to correct. I stood there and listened and gave them whatever piece of advice I felt could help get them through their situation. I always kept in the back of mind that I had gone through many of the similar situations they were going through and were probably afraid to raise their hand in class or to go and ask their peers for some advice out of fear they would be laughed at or to be called stupid. Especially when they reached the high school level because that's an entirely different beast where everyone is trying to build different relationships with their buddies and with the other gender. I always had students or athletes come to me for advice or ideas when it came to buying things like flowers and birthday gifts for their girlfriends or would ask me what I would do if I were in their shoes and was facing their situations.

One time, I had an incident where one of my best players had been in a relationship with his girlfriend dating back to 8th grade and it lasted all the way to their senior year, and she decided to end their relationship. You would have thought he had lost his mother as devastated as he was. I had to do everything in my power to get him through that rough and emotional time in his life to make sure that he was going to be alright. I had to put my arm around him and tell him that everything was going to be ok. I always wanted the student/athletes that I worked with to know that they had someone in their corner to turn to whenever they needed someone to talk to regardless of the situation they were facing. There were countless times when they would come back to me and thank me for helping them get them through their difficult times. As a teacher and a coach, I had always felt that's what we were there for. And for whatever reason, God gave me that gift of building relationships with the youth.

I will always remember my 9th grade year back when I had moved to the south side. I had just received my yearbook and there was a student named Karen Cox who came over to me and asked me if she could sign my yearbook. Of course, I didn't have a problem with her signing it, but for whatever reason, she wrote

"John is gonna help little kids in the world". At the time, I couldn't understand why she would even write that. I figured maybe it was just the nicest thing she could come up with. Karen ended up dying in a tragic car accident when she was just 19 years old. Here I am now at the age of 66 and I'm saying to myself, *"man that was a powerful statement that Karen had written for me"* because it ended up being the truth. It was almost as if she could look into the future and predict what I was here for. Who would have ever known. To me, Karen has always been an Angel now for the past 50 years. She left me something very valuable before she passed away. Her statement became very accurate and that's how I want to summarize who and what I was as a person working with the youth.

During the time I had been coaching and teaching at Corning Painted Post Schools District., I had also been working at Club Nautilus which became New York Sport and Fitness. I worked there from 1998 to 2014 to supplement my income to help pay for my son Michael's travel hockey league. After I had already retired from coaching and teaching, the school district's superintendent had the school district's personnel secretary call to ask if I would come back if they were able to create a position for me. They wanted me to come in as a liaison between the principal and the teachers to help students stay on the right track and help them with their behavior. I decided to go back and work at Winfield Elementary School which was the school where I had done some of my college prep work. I worked there for a year and a half before being asked by the School District's Superintendent to work over at Calvin U. Smith Elementary which is where I had begun my teaching career. While working there, I noticed that they had Calvin, our stuffed animal that we had at the Cougar's Den, was at the top of a shelf in the library. As soon as I saw it up there, I went and took it down, dusted him off and gave him a big ole' hug. They have since renovated and ended up building an addition at the school where they put Calvin behind a glass case which I can't wait to go and see. There were still a few teachers there that I had worked with, and I even ran into John Castiglione who had come in to visit along with a few other retired teachers that I hadn't seen in a very long time. It felt so good because I felt I had done a full circle.

I ended up making the decision to retire from teaching and coaching in 2015. It was a tough decision for me to make, but I knew I was ready. The district knew that I was sort of an icon and did try to talk me into staying, but I want to begin a new chapter in my life. There was never a feeling of me being tired of what I was doing or ever regretting any of it. I loved every bit of being a teacher and a coach all the way up until the very last minute. Even to this day I know that I could still go back and coach high school baseball. I know I can throw batting practice and develop a team and a program because I still have the passion and fire for it. But I was ready to venture out into the fitness world where I controlled the environment and was no longer locked into all the state rules and regulations. Not because they ever affected the way I coached, but I just wanted more freedom of working in a studio setting where I could continue to work with student/athletes and still make an impact on them. Because not only did we train by lifting weights and doing many different workouts, but we were also building great relationships the same way I did while I was coaching baseball.

I know I must have done a great job during my years of coaching because I eventually ended up being inducted into the Corning Painted Post Sports Hall of Fame just one year after I retired. Normally it would take five years after you retire to qualify, but the administrators felt that the job I had done throughout the years was great enough to not have to wait that long. It was a very powerful ending to my career, but I owe all of that to all the players and parents who were also there with me throughout my journey. I will always remember when our Athletic Director Tim Decker, who was a great friend of mine, passed away and I had our baseball team wear their warmup uniforms to the funeral to honor him. I was later told by our superintendent that if there was ever a Mt Rushmore for coaching in the Corning Painted Post School District that I would be on it. That really meant a lot to me because they all knew how much I loved coaching.

Do I have all the answers? No, I don't feel I do. But I have years of experience where I have witnessed many situations that should never occur in not just the sport of baseball, but in sports period. There's a message that I have that I want to get out there that I feel is damn powerful for students/athletes and parents/coaches because I feel that the direction most sports are heading today is pretty chaotic. I have witnessed some absurd behaviors to the point where I would ask myself *"do kids really have to go home to that?"* I could only imagine how those parents would deal with any other situations basing it on the way they were acting over just a game. It really saddens me to have to see that because it would always bring back old memories of when I had to deal with it myself. I truly believe that most of us in this world go through similar situations. But in the end, it's all about how you overcome them.

I reminisce often about my thirty-one years as a coach and think to myself sometimes that coaching was just as important on the field as it was off it. They were also very interesting when it came to dealing with situations that caused me to go from being a coach one minute to becoming a counselor and even dentist the next. But it didn't end there. Prior to me ever becoming a coach. I had wanted to continue playing baseball, but as we all know, life just happens. In my years of coaching, I had seven former players I coached get drafted in the major league baseball draft. Those seven players were just on a different level that separated them from the rest. Their work ethic, their approach for the game, they basically had God given talent. But at the end of the day, I treated everyone fair and loved every single one of them equally. There were many others who went on to do many great things in life. Some joined the military while others became doctors or chose other great professions. Baseball was just a small part of their lives but having them as my players was a blessing for me because they made my coaching career memorable. Baseball became such a big part of my life. What's crazy is how everything worked out for me as a coach. What started out as a job became one of my greatest achievements.

The game of baseball is pretty much based on failure. For you to overcome it and become successful, you have to go through the struggles, just like you have to do in life. The difference is, if you fail seven times out of ten in baseball, you could become a millionaire superstar in the Major Leagues. Now imagine there being a batting average when it comes to life. If you have those types of numbers when it comes to failing, you'll probably be considered worthless or a loser. My story of baseball and personal life pretty much ran parallel. I feel I went through many of my dealings in my early life and was given an opportunity to help my students and athletes get through theirs. I wish I could say it was a plan for me to do that, but like Kathy said to me that day when my players brought me my jersey from the equipment room, it had just been my *calling* all along.

ACKNOWLEDGMENTS

*"Surround yourself with people that push you to do better. No drama or negativity. Just higher goals and higher motivation. Good times and positive energy. No jealousy or hate. Simply bringing out the best in each other." - **Warren Buffett***

During my adolescence/adulthood years from 1970-1988 if someone said to me, *"John you will be a highly successful coach, educator, mentor, and author with 30 years of experience cumulating in a Hall of Fame induction in 2016"*, I would have questioned their mental stability. After all, my journey began in a totally dysfunctional family home life moving into several rental houses/apartments and surviving the trail and tribulations you face daily living in those elements. Through the journey, I met several individuals who had a very powerful impact on me and helped shape my values systems without the awareness or understanding. The first person I must acknowledge is my wife of 44 years Kathy for standing by me as my guardian angel throughout this journey. She has been in my life for 50 years exemplifying passionate charm, understanding beliefs, and the love for family are a few of her character traits. Kathy strong support and incredible ability of listening to my sometimes-quirky ideas are truly a gift. I am a firm believer that God sends you that one angel who guides you through the obstacles and roadblocks in life and my gift came in the name of Kathryn Marie Bradley/Knapp.

The next acknowledge is for Coach Dick Senko, coach, mentor, teacher, friend, for the nickname you gave me Knapper Snapper, that built our relationship, and for recognizing my baseball ability. Also, thank you for the rides and conversation we had on the way to the Corner of Harper and Oak Street while you were heading to German Street to see your girlfriend and future bride Eileen. Hat/Chest/ Ear our indicator, the signs Skin (steal), Cross arm across the chest (hit/run), Cross arm across the chest with skin (Squeeze play) on the JV team were the same indicator and signs I used throughout my thirty years coaching high school baseball. Thank you, Coach! I hope I made you proud!

The next professional I need to acknowledge would be Mr. Bill Kinney, a business law teacher at Elmira Southside. You provided me with rides and transportation during my junior and senior years while I attended Elmira Southside High School. The next influencer in my life was John Castiglione who was an outstanding leader and principal at Calvin U. Smith Elementary School in Painted- Post, New York. Thank you for believing in me. Acknowledgement to Mr. Lou Condon and Bill Thomas who were the two varsity baseball coaches at Corning East/West High School during my tenures as their junior varsity baseball coach and then promoted to the varsity ranks at Corning East High School when Bill retired! Their knowledge and wisdom of coaching high school baseball is second to none. Thank you, Bill and Lou!

Thank you and my sincere acknowledgment to Mr. Luis Martinez. Luis and I started this journey back in February of 2023. He provided me with professional expertise and incite to becoming an author. Also, Luis came into my life as my mother was struggling mentally and physically and eventually leaving this great place called earth and entering the gates of heaven. Thank you for your sincere blessing and support as I struggled with her passing.

A sincere thank you to Dr. Tony Branch for the uplifting words of encouragement to keep grinding my passion of helping others especially the student/athletes. Dr. Branch, my friend and brother from the day we met in Los Angeles on December 5th, 2015, you have provided me with spiritual and professional knowledge that strengthen my desire to write this book and tell my story. Most importantly, thanks for "YOUR TIME" throughout the past 7 years of mentoring.

Finally, I want to thank the many friends and family members along my journey who left an everlasting footprint imbedded in me. Too numerous to mention, but I will always remember the conversations we had and the outpouring of love and support you all gave me.

Made in the USA
Middletown, DE
28 August 2023

37405517R00080